simple stunning PARTIES at home

RECIPES, IDEAS, AND INSPIRATIONS FOR CREATIVE ENTERTAINING

KAREN BUSSEN

Photographs by **William Geddes**

STEWART, TABORI & CHANG | NEW YORK

**Dedicated with all my love to
Malik Abdur-Razzaq**

Published in 2009 by Stewart, Tabori & Chang
An imprint of Harry N. Abrams, Inc.

Cover location: A Condominiums
(see page 202 for contact information)

Library of Congress Cataloging-in-Publication Data

Bussen, Karen.
    Simple stunning parties at home : recipes, ideas,
and inspirations for creative entertaining / Karen
Bussen.
        p. cm.
    Includes index.
    ISBN 978-1-58479-674-9
1. Entertaining. 2. Cookery. 3. Parties. 4. Menus.
    I. Title.
TX731.B87 2009
642'.4—dc22   2008043283

Editor: Jennifer Levesque
Designer: Susi Oberhelman
Production Manager: Tina Cameron

The text of this book was composed in Helvetica Neue
and New Caledonia

Printed and bound in China

10 9 8 7 6 5 4 3 2 1

HNA ■■■■■
harry n. abrams, inc.
a subsidiary of La Martinière Groupe

115 West 18th Street
New York, NY 10011
www.hnabooks.com

contents

introduction

I believe we should all celebrate more often. In my work planning and designing hundreds of parties, I have been a witness to many important moments and special memories in the lives of all kinds of people.

Most of the parties my company creates are larger celebrations—weddings, anniversaries, milestone birthdays, and other major moments. I've noticed that the nature of these much-anticipated special occasions seems to encourage people to appreciate each other openly. They have permission to put aside their differences for a few hours, to laugh and talk and feast together. They gain a sense of life's preciousness and their own good fortune, a feeling that a place in time is being held just for them.

But in between these big moments, which are approached with more formality, there are plenty of daily opportunities to celebrate. And as I always say, when opportunity knocks, answer the door and offer it some Champagne!

My company designs and plans incredible parties. For this beautiful wedding celebration just ouside of New Orleans, we set a 150-foot-long table, so that every guest could sit with the bride and groom.

Whereas a larger, more structured gathering such as a wedding might require a special venue and fancy catering, a home, being the center of our daily lives, is the perfect place to create a beautiful mosaic of intimate, vibrant moments and memories with friends and family.

Entertaining at home is a very personal activity, and each gathering you host should be a reflection of your own gracious style, whether it's a holiday feast or a quick after-work get-together for wine and cheese. And while perfection is not the goal, it's amazing how sprinkling in just a few creative details will help make your next party at home even more memorable.

There is always a reason to celebrate, in my opinion, whether it's the change in seasons or a new job or just the fact that I like wine! But of course we all live in the real world of work, family, errands, projects, and all the other commitments that compete for our time. With that in mind, I've filled this book with a dozen simple, beautiful party ideas to help inspire you. I've divided them into four categories—Cocktail Gatherings, Casual Suppers, Dinner Parties, and a section of one-off get-togethers (a Brunch, a Lunch & a Linner).

When my staff and I create a party for one of our clients, we hold brainstorming meetings to devise a plan for each aspect of the celebration. We start with the big picture, talking about the mood we want to evoke. Then we fill in the details, thinking about ways to add magic with music, flowers, lighting, food, drinks, and entertainment. Could the ballroom doors suddenly fly open during dinner to reveal a marching band in full formation? Might we hire a local artist to paint a portrait of guests enjoying a wedding feast?

Our goal is to make each event a one-of-a-kind experience. We talk through timing and flow, imagining how guests will transition between cocktails and dinner, and how we'll keep building the energy of the party with surprises big and small. Soon we have a "recipe" for a fabulous event, and we use it to do our designing, shopping, and production.

I apply a similar approach to entertaining in my own home, albeit on a much smaller scale. (I typically forego marching bands in my apartment in favor of a good iPod mix.)

When it comes to my personal parties, I tend to plan on a very short time line (like, "I have a day off? Let's have a party—tomorrow!"), and I am not the type to sit at home for weeks knitting napkin rings or making chair covers out of fresh flowers. It's just not my style. I'd rather come up with simple and fresh ideas that feel easy and effortless, like using a giant leaf as a placemat or repurposing objects (old bowls, glass jars, etc.) into clever centerpieces or displays.

Also, I am almost always on a tighter budget than my clients, so I try to think of creative alternatives to the more luxe options (serving wine spritzers instead of Champagne, for example). But I still use the "party recipe" process to help me bring all the elements together.

So that's the way I've designed the parties you'll find here. Each one has a mixture of ideas to help you put it all together—menu, drinks, décor, music, and extra details. In the back, you'll find the food and drink recipes collected so you can easily search for inspirations for your next party or for any night of the week. In addition, I've thrown in some tips for last-minute dishes you can make when you're in a time crunch. I've also provided recipes for the nine cocktails I think every great host should know how to make.

There are chapters to help you prepare to be a great host, with tips on how to create a party pantry and how to stock a home bar for entertaining. I've included a section on creating the perfect atmosphere and a few ideas for gifts for guests and hosts, which I hope you'll try.

Finally, I'd like to say a word about the simple stunning approach. The point of this book is not to encourage flawless home entertaining. Rather, it's an invitation to celebrate life more often and to spend time with people you care for, toasting and tasting the wonderful flavors nature (and your kitchen) have to offer. The simple stunning vibe is just that—it highlights the "less-is-more" approach to décor, limiting colors for more visual impact and limiting

waste wherever possible. Simple stunning party menus feature wonderful ingredients in straightforward preparations to let flavors sing. And our projects combine homemade and store-bought items in fresh, easy, and elegant presentations.

A note on Going Green: The popular trend toward becoming more environmentally friendly is fantastic, and it's right in line with the simple stunning philosophy. I created my party business to offer design alternatives for folks who wanted a less over-the-top ambience for their celebrations.

We make it a priority to reuse, recycle, and regift whenever we can. Whether we're creating dual uses for design elements (repurposing reception flowers as centerpieces for a brunch the next day) or donating no-longer-needed props and materials to local schools and arts organizations, we are committed to doing our part to help decrease waste. We continue to seek out resources and vendors to help us become more ecofriendly, so in that spirit, I've tried to share an easy idea or two here and there in this book if you'd like to do the same.

Entertaining at home can and should be enjoyable enough to make you want to do it more often. So raise a glass, grab some inspiration, and let's get this party started!

love long tables! Guests dined under the stars, on the oak-tree studded front lawn of the gorgeous historic Houmas House.

advice for THE HOST

When it comes to flowers in the home, there is nothing more beautiful—or easy to create—than a dramatic mass of just one type of blossom, like these fragrant, lush lilacs.

Stress doesn't bother me when I'm planning a huge, important event for someone else. I have been in some pretty crazy situations related to the parties I create (everything from missing silk tablecloths for a gala honoring members of a certain royal family to thousand-pound flower arrangements flipping over in the wind, from cancelled weddings to bickering families—even small fires and medical emergencies), but I'm always pretty calm and collected.

However, when I'm hosting my own party, I worry just like everyone else (or maybe worse). I want it to be perfect, I want to dazzle my guests with delicious food and fabulous details, and I want everyone to have a super-fun experience.

The exciting idea of creating a party at home tends to become a stressful prospect when you start to imagine everything you "have to do." You "have to" cook from scratch, decorate beautifully, and make sure your house is in perfect order. Pretty soon, the very sight of your to-do list has you asking why you got yourself into this mess and worrying that you won't be able to pull it together.

I've been there many times. I've experienced the joy (and the pain) of planning hundreds of parties, for both clients and loved ones, and frankly, the joy part is *way* more fun. After all, the whole point of entertaining, especially entertaining at home, is to create fun for you and your guests! So below I've shared some of the tips and tricks that have helped me organize, imagine, and just think differently about the idea of hosting a great celebration while having a great time in the process.

Prepare to party. A little planning goes a long way. Whether you want to host more formal dinners with friends or you just want to make it easier to have folks over on short notice, stocking a home bar and "party pantry" lets you pull an event

like to have a drink and a nibble ready to go as soon as guests arrive, and sangria is always a hit. To keep big batches of drinks from getting watery, I make them without ice, chill the pitcher, then add ice when I'm ready to serve.

together with less running around and more time for a bubble bath before people arrive! See page 19 for more details on creating your party pantry.

Welcome your guests with food and drink. Have a simple, delicious hors d'oeuvre and a glass of wine waiting for them near the door or on a kitchen counter when they arrive. This way, if you have any last-minute preparations to make, they can visit with you—or each other—while enjoying a snack and a sip.

Create a party circle. Share the toasting and the hosting. Get a group of friends and neighbors together and start a moving feast or cocktail event that happens once a month at a different host's home. Choose a recurring theme such as the Wine & Cheese Tasting (page 48) or the Global Potluck supper (page 66), and alternate regions or flavors, or combine a book club meeting and dinner party, with the evening's flavors inspired by your current literary selection or author.

Try new things, but not all at once. If you're like me, you probably enjoy experimenting with new ideas for drinks, recipes, even décor. But doing too much can make for stress in the hours leading up to your guests' arrival. My advice: don't be a hero. Try one or two new things for each party, supplementing with more familiar elements (a classic cocktail or a family recipe). To track your successes, keep a party journal. Write down what works and which ideas are favorites, and you'll begin building a great repertoire of party inspirations.

the Union Square Greenmarket is one of New York City's best places to find fresh produce and other artisanal ingredients. To find seasonal markets in your area, visit www.farmersmarket.com

Use high-quality ingredients. Whenever possible, cook with seasonal items and buy organic ingredients from local purveyors and farmers. This not only supports your regional economy and the environment—it also helps ensure that your finished dishes will be more healthful and delicious. Get to know the best resources in your area and use them to enhance your favorite recipes for parties and everyday cooking. If you do a little research, you may find a local farmers' cooperative, or an old grist mill that grinds flour daily, or a butcher who specializes in organic meats. More and more grocery stores are also heeding the call to offer healthful, ecofriendly alternatives, so you might see some great products very close to home. For all the recipes in this book, you can assume that wherever possible and unless I've noted otherwise, I'm recommending seasonal, organic ingredients.

Don't be afraid to substitute. Fresh is wonderful, but sometimes not possible. Some of the recipes in this book call for frozen or canned items, or even store-bought mixes. Sometimes an alternative ingredient is just a smarter choice. For example, in my opinion, using frozen spinach for Creamed Spinach Royale is not only easier than boiling down giant pots of fresh leaves—both the yield and the texture of the frozen spinach are better. The point is, I'm not saying you should never eat a strawberry out of season—just use the best of what you have available and make the most of it!

Apply the "less waste, more taste" principle. I have a friend whose mom always used to say that before leaving the house we should take a look in the mirror and remove one accessory. This applies to many aspects of party planning, from the use of color to limiting your menu to filling a space with too much stuff. There's nothing like a well-edited room or a simple, beautiful table setting. Being a bit more environmentally friendly does not mean you can never buy a new set of plates or send out a party invitation. Just be aware of ways you can conserve and preserve. Try to use recycled glass or sustainable materials (bamboo platters, soy candles, and so on) whenever you can. Shop with reusable totes. Resist the temptation to overdecorate. Wrap up leftovers and give them to guests to enjoy later. Host a Regift Exchange Brunch (page 94) and swap items you don't use.

Say it again: "Perfection is overrated." The best parties I've given (and attended) have not

hint

AN INVITATION TO BE CREATIVE

For most parties at home, I recommend keeping your invitations casual and easy. A phone call will do nicely, as will a simple handwritten or computer printed card, or an e-invitation via one of the great Internet sites such as evite.com or bluemountain.com.

If you like to do craft projects, you can always get more elaborate. Certainly for a formal party (like our New Year's Eve fête on page 86), you might want to do something special. If so, I recommend keeping some basic tools on hand, such as a variety of rubber stamps, decorative scissors, monogram stickers, and other accents. I have a file filled with pretty paper remnants, which I use to make quick invites and greeting cards. But if the idea of having to create something from scratch is holding you back from having a great party, you should skip fancy papers and text everyone to "get here now!"

hint

USE IT OR LOSE IT

Another argument for using the good stuff: Did you know that fine silver tarnishes much faster when it sits unused? If you enjoy it on a regular basis, it won't need constant polishing. Just don't put it in the dishwasher!

been the ones that were flawless. They were the gatherings that happened at the last minute, when friends dropped by without giving me the time to design a fabulous centerpiece or wax my floor. Then there was the time when I burnt the pork chops, so we had fun whipping up drinks and an impromptu supper with whatever I had in the house. There is a certain charm and style to happy imperfection. If you can remember that, you'll enjoy entertaining (and life in general) so much more!

your party PANTRY

these are a few of my favorite things—white plates and napkins, pretty glasses, colorful votives, and simple pillar candles. Combining basics with unique accents lets you tailor your table to your occasion and theme.

Part of the secret to hosting great parties at home is having the tools you need within easy reach. Think of yourself as a party artist and put together a palette of unique accents to help inspire you and make your home entertaining easier, even at the last minute.

In my apartment, I've organized what I call a "party pantry"—it's a shelving unit divided into cubes. I use it to store special plates, Champagne glasses, serving pieces, my fondue pot, different types of vases, and candles. I keep colorful place mats there and napkins in varying hues to accent my basic china, which is white and very simple. When it's time to throw a dinner party or a wine and cheese night on the spur of the moment, I look here for design inspiration, and I pull together all the elements I need. Because my apartment is rather small, this special space functions dually as a beautiful spot to display my favorite party accessories and as a much-needed extra storage area.

Look at your home and find a place to help organize the tools you need for home entertaining. It could be a small closet, a cupboard in the kitchen, or an antique hutch—whatever works for you.

getting started

Once you have chosen a space for your party pantry, I suggest you begin by stocking it with basic pieces such as dinner plates and a few serving platters in white. Most chefs would agree that, in general, food looks best on a simple white plate, and the versatility of white makes it a wonderful tool for changing the look of your table. Just add a few colorful elements (such as place mats, runners, and napkins) and you can create many different moods.

Add texture and visual power to your party palette by focusing on two or three types of materials

accents are everything. While I prefer to drink wine out of clear glasses, I love to use colorful goblets (above) and flutes for cocktails, water, or champagne. A collection of fun napkin rings offers inspiration for a festive table (opposite).

tip

SERVING IT UP

You can never have enough platters and oversized bowls. Collect them as you find ones you like, gathering an assortment in simple white, along with a few colorful or unique accent pieces to complement your party arsenal!

for accent pieces. Build up your party pantry over time, shopping when things are on sale throughout the year rather than at the last minute when a shortage of time can cause you to choose something you don't really love (and to pay more for it). Consider adding a few flea-market finds (an antique vase or teapot) or an artsy candlestick or basket that you can use often.

what to look for

Here are some tips for picking the right materials, colors, and items for your party pantry. Choose things that will work well with the interior design of your home and your own style preferences.

Mood	Materials/Colors	Start with These Pieces
Earthy, Natural	Handcrafted wood (teak, acacia) and ceramic, recycled glass, and fabric accents in cotton or linen (focus on a palette of neutral and warm colors like sage, chocolate, and khaki)	Serving bowls, platters, beeswax or soy candles, and woven grass place mats
Exotic	Sleek lacquer, painted bamboo, boldly patterned ceramics, and fabrics in neutrals or warm reds, deep jewel tones, and metallics	Trays and small bowls, chopsticks, spicy scented candles, jeweled or tasseled napkin rings, and throw pillows
Modern	Glass, ceramic, resin, and stainless steel; cool colors such as frosty white and charcoal, with accents in any color you like; fabrics in simple geometric patterns	Plates, vases, and votive candleholders in simple, geometric shapes, and mirror tiles for coasters or a runner
Heirloom	Porcelain, silver, cut crystal—simple colors and patterns mixed with eclectic florals, textured borders, and bold stripes	Candlestick holders, a vintage coffee service, silver napkin rings, a fine tablecloth, and charger plates

foods for your party pantry

In addition to serving pieces and decorative elements, I like to keep certain store-bought food items on hand in my party pantry. These are snacks and condiments I can break out on a moment's notice when friends drop by. Here are a few of my favorites:

- Packaged plain breadsticks (see my recipe for dressing them up on page 136)
- Jars of olives, pickled jalapeños, stuffed grape leaves, and roasted sweet peppers
- Pistachios and mixed nuts or trail mixes
- Dill pickles
- Bottles of my favorite pasta sauce (in case I don't have time to make my own) and a few types of pasta (penne, linguine, cavatappi)
- Boxes of crispbreads and crackers
- A variety of unusual chips (root vegetable, pita, tortilla, and others)
- Dried fruits (apricots, cranberries, cherries, and golden raisins)
- Plain microwave popcorn
- Dried Italian sausages and salami
- Biscotti or other cookies

these glass vases hold just one or two blooms each, but when grouped together, they create a dramatic centerpiece.

hint

A TOUCH OF GREEN

More and more homeware companies are offering plates, platters, and other essentials in handcrafted artisan designs and environmentally friendly materials such as recycled glass, bamboo, and rapidly renewable woods. See page 115 for some websites to check out if you're interested in adding a handmade touch or a little green to your party pantry.

raising THE BAR

When can I move in? This simple stunning bar is stocked with everything a home bartender needs to sip, and serve, in style, including aperitifs, unique wines and spirits, and great glassware.

Tell me, who among us does not imagine having a dream bar in their home? A chic, well-stocked, advantageously lit nook where one can wet one's whistle, gather with friends, and get shaken and stirred? Bond, *Karen* Bond.

Well, by now you probably know that my apartment is smallish, so my home bar is just a section of my party pantry filled with my favorite aperitifs, liquors, and mixers, along with a couple of cocktail shakers, some pitchers, and a few good bartending books for inspiration and instruction. My freezer doubles as the perfect storage facility for icy-cold vodka, and I love any kind of gadget that lets me open wine without pulling a muscle or breaking a nail, so I have a drawer full of those items.

If you are lucky enough to have a fabulous area, decked out and dedicated to festive libations, please invite me over immediately. If, like me, you are space-challenged, check out some of my tips for what you need and how you can organize a user-friendly home bar to make your own mixing and mingling much more fun.

bar essentials

Whether your home bar is a fabulous built-in counter or a simple roll-away cart, filling it with a few essentials can make throwing a party much easier and will surely save you some last-minute trips to the store. Here are some ideas to help you raise the bar at your next get-together.

If you plan to serve cocktails, you'll need a few basic tools:

- A cocktail shaker with strainer top (to prevent ice from getting into drinks)
- A shot glass for measuring
- A long stirring spoon
- A bottle opener

Classic martini glasses are always in fashion, but adding a few splashy cocktail glasses is a great way to mix things up at your next soirée.

- A corkscrew for wine bottles
- Ice buckets for chilling bottles and tongs or a scoop for dispensing ice
- Garnishes and supplies
  - ‣ Olives, cocktail onions, cherries, limes, and lemons
  - ‣ Stir sticks, straws, toothpicks, and napkins
- A variety of glasses
  - ‣ Highballs—tall, narrow glasses that can be used for many drinks
  - ‣ Old-fashioned or "rocks" glasses—shorter and wider
  - ‣ Martini glasses—for "up" cocktails
  - ‣ Champagne flutes and wineglasses

other accents and tools of the trade

- Speed pourers (replace the caps on liquor bottles and make for speedier mixing)
- A muddler (used to mash fruit and other elements, such as mint, for certain special cocktails)
- Coasters to protect furniture
- A blender, if you like to make frozen drinks
- A good bartender's guide to cocktail recipes
- Specialty glasses (snifters for brandy, cordial glasses for port and dessert wine, margarita glasses)

liquor and mixers

THE BASICS

- Vodka (the most popular liquor for mixed drinks)
- Rum (light for fruity drinks, dark for the Dark & Stormy on page 186)
- Tequila (younger *blanco* varieties for mixing, *reposado* or *anejo* for sipping)
- Scotch (blended for mixed drinks, single malts for purists)
- Whiskey (there are many choices—I'd start with a good bourbon such as Booker's or Knob Creek for sipping and a rye whiskey such as Canadian Club for mixed drinks)
- Dry and sweet vermouth (for martinis and other cocktails)
- Club soda, tonic water, cola, and a lemon-lime soda, plus Rose's Lime Juice
- Juices (orange, cranberry, lime, and grapefruit)

OPTIONAL

- Lillet Blanc (an orange-infused French aperitif)
- Gin (for classic martinis and gimlets—I adore Hendrick's, a cucumber-and-rose-infused gin from Scotland)
- Peychaud's Bitters (from New Orleans, this herbal concoction is a staple for my favorite retro whiskey cocktail, the Sazerac, see page 186)
- Grand Marnier (an orange-flavored brandy)
- Ginger beer or ginger ale
- Crème de cassis (a black currant–flavored liqueur)
- Simple syrup (see page 185 for the recipe)
- Amaretto (a sweet, almond-flavored liqueur)
- Dry Sherry (great with cheese and nuts)

CHOOSING YOUR GARNISHES

Before your party, decide which cocktails you'd like to offer and purchase only those perishable garnishes you really need. Mint for mojitos and sakejitos, limes for margaritas and vodka drinks, lemon twists for Sazeracs and martinis, along with the other classic martini garnishes—cocktail onions and olives. Maraschino cherries are a must only if you'll serve sweet drinks such as Manhattans, and wedges of orange, blood orange, clementine, or pineapple are perfect for tropical drinks.

I love to offer interesting aperitifs before a dinner party, such as Lillet Blanc with a splash of club soda and an orange slice. Experiment with new flavors and start building your own collection.

dessert wines

There are so many choices for post-meal libations. Here are a few notes to get you started.

PORT

Port is wine fortified with brandy. There are numerous varieties at many price points. Generally, ruby and tawny versions are the most economical and least full bodied (although all ports are relatively intense in flavor), with late-bottle-vintage and vintage bottlings being the most complex and the priciest. If you like big red wines and a bit of sweetness, you may love port, especially in the colder months. Try it with hearty cheeses, nuts, figs, dates, and even poached fruits.

SWEET DESSERT WINE

Many sweet wines are made with grapes that are harvested late (they are allowed to remain on the vine longer to concentrate the sugar content in the grapes), and they are sometimes dried before being made into wine. There is a whole world of sweet wines to try, so if you're interested, start with an Italian Vin Santo or Malvasia delle Lipari and work your way up to a French Sauternes or even a Hungarian Tokaji. These highly concentrated wines feature varying flavors and aromas (dried fruit, honey, flowers) and are best paired with simple desserts, like cookies, biscotti, or mild cakes and fruit. They can also be wonderful with a variety of cheeses and nuts.

glass decanters are used for two purposes—separating a wine from any sediment in the bottle, and letting a wine "breathe," so that its flavors and aromas can open up.

SPARKLING DESSERT WINE

I love a dessert wine with bubbles, and I have to say the Italians make two of my favorites—Moscato d'Asti with its flavors of fresh peaches and its floral aromas, and Brachetto Acqui, the dramatic red sparkler with its berry freshness and big bubbles. Of course, I'd never turn my back on a great demi-sec (off-dry) Champagne with a creamy French Brie or Saint André cheese.

other after-dinner drinks

In addition to wines, there are also spirited options to choose from—mellow armagnacs and elegant cognacs from France and other brandies from around the world. Or sample Italy's grappa, but be ready for a kick!

purchasing wine for your party

The average bottle of wine is 750 milliliters and yields about five glasses of wine, or about ten "tastes." Deciding exactly how much wine to buy for a party can be difficult, as of course some folks prefer other beverages. But in general, here are a few guidelines to help you plan. If you're ever in

WHICH WINEGLASSES SHOULD YOU BUY?

If you're a budding connoisseur, start with something basic that will work for both white and red wine. I recommend clear glass, as appreciating a wine's color is a part of the tasting process. A tulip-shaped, Bordeaux-style glass is a solid choice, and I suggest picking a style that's on the larger side, so that you'll have room to swirl your wine in the glass before smelling and tasting it.

When you're ready, and when you know more about which wines you like to drink most often, investing in high-quality glasses is a great idea. Consult with a professional in a good home retail store for advice on which glasses are right for you and consider the fact that some of the best wineglasses are delicate and must be hand-washed to avoid breakage.

doubt, just purchase a few extra bottles. You can always enjoy them later.

- **For a cocktail party** where other spirits will be served, I suggest ordering one bottle of wine for every three guests.
- **For a wine and cheese tasting,** count on needing a bottle of wine for every two guests. So, for a wine tasting for twelve guests, you'd need six bottles of wine in total. You can divide that into six different wines for small tastes, or choose two bottles each of three different wines.
- **The same is true for a dinner party**—plan on one bottle of wine per every two guests.

Of course, as I mentioned, it never hurts to have a couple of extra bottles on hand, and if you find a wine you particularly like, you can typically get a discount for purchasing by the case. Just open the bottles you need as you go, and keep any leftovers for next time.

Want to find out about tastings and wine happenings in your area? Check out one of my favorite websites, www.localwineevents.com, and follow links to your state and city.

how to choose wines for a party

It's important to think about what you'll be eating when you're choosing wines for any celebration. There are many schools of thought about how to pair wines, but a good rule of thumb is, for a cocktail party, choose lighter, less complex wines.

WINE AND FOOD PAIRINGS TO TRY

Most of the suggestions below are listed by grape name. Some of them are place names of particular wines (Châteauneuf-du-Pape, for example, is the name of a wine blended from as many as thirteen grapes). If you're unsure how to look for these wines, visit a good retail shop and ask for more information about which vintages and producers to try. And if you're really interested in learning more, I suggest you subscribe to a good magazine that focuses on wine and food such as *Wine Spectator* or *Food & Wine*. You can also spend some time browsing online at the many informative wine websites or sign up for a class in your area and have fun sipping.

- **Light seafood:** Vouvray, Sauvignon Blanc, Pinot Blanc, Sancerre, Verdicchio
- **Spicy seafood or chicken:** Gewürztraminer, Riesling, Chardonnay, Dolcetto d'Alba, Beaujolais
- **Light pastas and salads:** Pinot Grigio, Sauvignon Blanc, Orvieto, or a refreshing rosé Côtes du Rhône or Tavel

- **Pork and lighter meat dishes:** Rose Rioja Barbera, Pinot Noir, Côtes du Rhône, Tempranillo
- **Lamb and stewed meats:** Cabernet Sauvignon, Valpolicella, Gigondas, Rioja, Zinfandel
- **Fuller-flavored meats and game:** Barolo, Barbaresco, Châteauneuf-du-Pape, Amarone, Bordeaux, Shiraz

STORAGE

Keep your wines calm and cool. White wines are best stored between 50°F and 55°F. Red "cellar temperature" is slightly warmer, between 55°F and 60°F. If you don't have room to refrigerate all your wines, just keep them in a cool place, away from strong light and sudden temperature changes.

SERVING

When ready to serve, consider these guidelines:

- Chill crisp whites to between 35°F and 40°F.
- Serve bigger whites at 55°F.
- Offer reds at a cool, but not chilled, 65°F for best results.

NEXT LEVEL!

For serious oenophiles, a wine refrigerator can be a much-coveted accessory. You can store wines at room temperature, but keeping them slightly chilled can help protect them from sudden fluctuations that can damage corks and ruin flavors.

EMILY

友
Friend

What are you
most thankful
FOR ?

creating AMBIENCE

Simple details make your table shine. This homemade paper napkin ring provides both a personal welcome and a conversation-starter at dinner.

When you create a party, you create a mood. Think about the mood you envision for your next fête. Spicy? Serene? Elegant? Exotic? Let all the elements of your celebration—food, drinks, music, color, even lighting—harmonize to create just the right atmosphere. You might be surprised how easy it is to transform your everyday space and take your party to the next level with a few tricks. Here are some of my favorite ideas for creating a wonderful environment. I use them when I'm planning and designing events on a grand scale, as well as when I'm having friends over at my place.

NEVER TOO MUCH

I tell all my clients, and I'll tell you too: There is no such thing as too many candles. Even in the summertime if you have no air conditioning, the soft glow of candlelight will make your hot, sweaty guests look like steamy, sexy golden gods and goddesses. Here are some pointers:

- If you're on a budget, hear this: Skip flowers and other fancy décor and buy white pillar, votive, and floating candles whenever you see them on sale.
- It can be hard to get hold of beautiful, ecofriendly soy candles at good prices, so keep an eye out for them.
- I love beeswax candles, with their incredible texture and their slightly sweet smell. Did you know if you keep beeswax candles in the refrigerator before burning them, they'll last longer?

When you're ready to party (or whenever you just need more mood), kick the atmosphere into the stratosphere—cluster your candles on coffee tables and counters, line windowsills with them, float them in glasses, and light them up. Of course it goes without saying, be careful and attentive, and never fall asleep while candles are burning. One last thought: Resist the temptation to put a candle on the top of your toilet tank—I've seen two long-haired, slightly tipsy gals get scorched!

nstant party. A tray filled with glowing gold candles makes a simple, gorgeous centerpiece, and these long-burning pillars can be reused to illuminate many a festive occasion.

Make space to mingle. Clear any clutter, making room to roam and providing adequate—but not excessive—seating for a cocktail hour. This will help keep the social energy bubbly, festive, and comfortable. For a casual get-together, add a few oversized throw pillows near a seating area to create a relaxed vibe.

Lighting is magic. No other element of décor makes more of an impact on the mood of a party. Think about it. Have you ever visited a chic night-club or romantic restaurant in the daytime? With the harsh overhead lights on, you see every flaw, and the spell is broken. When the lighting is right, people look and feel wonderful and the magic is in full effect. If your party is in the evening, I recommend that you eliminate overhead lighting and switch on floor and table lamps to create a textured glow throughout the space. (At my place, I even have countertop lamps in my kitchen, and I've permanently disabled the overhead fixtures!)

If you want even more mood, consider replacing bulbs here and there with softer rosy tones or more dramatic shades of red, amber, or blue. And, of course, the more candles placed in groups or in long rows on windowsills, the better.

If you're hosting a daytime event, let as much natural light into your space as possible—or just move the party outside into the sunshine! If you're having a daytime party on a rainy day, light a couple of scented candles in your home for a cozy feeling.

Use color as a tool. Like lighting, color is a transformative party design element. But you don't have to repaint your house or reupholster the couch to give your living space a new look. Adding a heap of colorful pillows to your couch or a bold runner and napkins to your dining table is an instant way to renew your space. Follow the simple stunning principle of color to make your party pop: Feel free to vary your color accents between rooms, but for the most design bang, highlight no more than three main colors in any party space. Mixing too many colors (unless you're in a garden) will lessen the impact of each.

Get fresh with your décor. Look around and see things in new ways. Flip silverware upside down. Mix and match plates. Make flower arrangements in teacups, cookie tins, or Champagne glasses. Turn a vase on its head and use it as a pedestal for a buffet. Using familiar things in new ways will delight your guests and showcase your personal style, which is what great parties are all about.

Invite new people. Of course we all have our short list of folks we like to invite to any get-together. But don't be afraid to invite new friends or acquaintances and seat couples or best friends separately at a dinner party. You and your guests might very well find your social network growing, and your parties will be filled with new people, new energy, and new ideas.

Keep a party journal. I keep a diary/folder handy for my parties at home. It's an inspirational gathering place for recipes and ideas I want to try, an organizer for my shopping lists and notes, and a scrapbook for labels from wines I like and menus or dishes that went over well. Sometimes I add in snapshots from the party to remind me how much fun it was. I love looking through this book, and every time I open it, I want to plan another party!

bright red napkins, flatware, and lanterns add a spicy touch to a plain picnic table (opposite). Stones help keep the wind at bay. Adorn your front door with inexpensive plants for a warm welcome (above.)

celebration

12 SIMPLE STUNNING PARTIES

inspiration

Want to throw a dinner or brunch at your place? Look at your schedule. It's busy, yes? But maybe there's a free evening or weekend coming up soon. If not, take my advice: Cancel something and have a party anyway! Celebrating is such an important part of life—make a little time for food and friends, and you'll be so happy you did.

But what kind of event should you put together? To help inspire you, I've captured a dozen parties on these pages. I've divided the celebrations into four categories. Many of the parties are perfect for different occasions—birthdays, anniversaries, networking, or a weeknight whim. There are some seasonal gatherings as well.

For each theme, there's a party "recipe" which includes a suggested menu, décor and music inspirations, and other ideas to make the party simple and stunning. Beginning on page 116, you'll find all the recipes for suggested menu items, but feel free to mix and match dishes from any parties you like.

All the party dishes and décor ideas are designed to be straight-forward, using limited ingredients and basic techniques. So go ahead, choose what you like and bring it to life. Then write down your favorites for future party inspiration.

The most important thing to remember about hosting a cocktail party is that *it's a cocktail party, not dinner.* It's meant to be easy to put together on short notice, a fun and relaxed get-together for your guests and you. Keep foods bite-size and packed with flavor, and if you want to serve something sweet at the end, make it simple and light. • I love to start cocktails earlier rather

cocktail gatherings

than later (if you're hosting on the weekend, I recommend beginning at five or so in the afternoon, as it allows for other plans afterward). For weeknights, it seems work schedules make it impossible for anyone to arrive much before six. But that still provides for ample party time and an early night for those who must work, or a dinner reservation at a reasonable hour for those night owls in your group.

latin spice

This sexy, chic, and simple evening is perfect for a special occasion (birthday, celebrating a promotion, etc.) or anytime you're just in the mood for some Latin flavor. And, tell me, who isn't in the mood for some Latin flavor right about now?

You'll notice that the food is nibble-friendly and designed to limit the need for lots of plates and silverware. The flavors are bold but can be tailored to your preferred spice levels. The recipes are easy, but if you're short on time or just want to make your preparations even easier, you can substitute store-bought salsa for the homemade version or purchase a high-quality premade margarita mix rather than making a big pitcher from scratch. Malik's Tropical Rosé Sangria is so quick and delicious—I highly recommend you make that one. You'll be the talk of the town!

We've arranged all the food buffet-style on a kitchen island, but you could use your dining table if that makes more sense. Another fresh idea is to place smaller groupings of food and drinks around your living and entertaining space, on coffee tables and sideboards, so guests discover them as they mingle.

When you think about décor for this party, keep it simple but unexpected. If you like flowers, just a few tropical blooms make an affordable, dramatic statement. I arranged a "collected" centerpiece with a single stem of "sexy pink" hanging heliconia, ten stems of orange protea "pincushion," and a handful of hot peppers.

NEXT LEVEL!

If you'd like to turn this Latin Spice theme into more of a dinner party, choose one or two of the hors d'oeuvres, then add Arroz con Pollo (page 143) as a main course. Serve the Banana Bites with vanilla ice cream or offer Strawberry Angel-Food Trifle (page 174) for a light end to the meal. For a sit-down dinner, I use Post-it note flags to arrange my seating plan.

the menu

- Go-to Guacamole & Homemade Fresh Salsa and chips
- Coconut Shrimp Ceviche
- Quick Quesadillas
- Manchego Jalapeño Cornbread
- Caramelized Cinnamon Banana Bites with vanilla ice cream

aperitifs/drinks

Dry sherry, Malik's Tropical Rosé Sangria, Margaritas Más Grandes, and Mexican beer (I like Dos Equis and El Presidente)

wines

Bubbly cava (a budget-friendly sparkler from Spain) or a spicy Riesling (although not Latin, flowery, exotic Riesling is a grape that pairs well with full-flavored foods)

music

Sexy, festive, and hot! Mix up slow and fast rhythms. Download sultry sambas and bossa novas and raucous salsa beats. Stir in a little tropical flavor with some fun Caribbean dance hall grooves or up-tempo reggae.

RECOMMENDED ARTISTS:

- **Salsa/Cuban:** Fruko y Sus Tesos, Tito Puente, Juan Luis Guerra, Celia Cruz, Afro-Cuban All Stars

extra!

Create a warm Latin-inspired welcome. Make Tequila-Soaked Olives with Blue Cheese (see page 137) and offer them, along with a bowl of salted almonds, on your foyer or coffee table. *Arriba!*

- **Samba/Bossa Nova:** Antonio Carlos Jobim, Astrud Gilberto, Quincy Jones
- **Reggae:** Bob Marley (and his son Damian Marley), Third World, Shabba Ranks, Sean Paul

décor

Liven up your party space with a palette of bold accent colors. Choose from citrus tones, deep reds, purples, and hot pinks. Arrange a single *gigante* bunch of red or orange roses (or just a huge bowl of oranges or peppers, if flowers aren't available) on your bar or hors d'oeuvres table. Buy a few accent pillows for your couch or floor. Create a welcome arrangement of hot red peppers, or preburn tall taper and pillar candles in mix-and-match holders—lighting them early lets the wax drip a little for a romantic, sexy vibe.

smokin' hot detail

If you host this party outdoors on a warm night, it might be fun to offer some good cigars with a mellow, sweet Brandy de Jerez.

wine & cheese tasting

This gourmet gathering is so simple, you can plan for it one day and host it the next! And while I'm suggesting mostly French cheeses and wines here, you can turn this party into a revolving get-together, say, once a month, hosting it at a different friend's house and choosing a new region (Portugal, Austria,

Napa Valley) or a new theme (World's Best Blue Cheeses and Big Red Wines, for example).

If you're a novice at matching wines and cheeses, plan your party menu with cheese and wine selections from the same place, such as Spain or Italy. Somehow, elements that grow together often go together, making wonderful worry-free pairings! If you love cheese and wine and want to learn more, check local cooking schools and your favorite wine-friendly restaurants for classes and events. In the Raising the Bar chapter, page 25, I've also listed websites to check out if you're interested.

To prepare for your party, visit a store that specializes in good cheeses and speak with a knowledgeable salesperson who will let you taste various cheeses and will give you hints for serving your selections to show them at their best.

Keep the food and presentation simple—we've used wooden cutting boards and chalkboards to present and identify our French cheeses. Put out different kinds of artisan breads—simple baguettes, a hearty raisin-nut loaf, and something with olives or onions, for example. Plates of crackers or crispbreads are also great. Fruit—fresh and dried—pairs beautifully with cheese. Look for ripe pears in season and, of course, lots of juicy grapes.

the menu

We picked six French cheeses of varying flavors, textures, and intensities and supplemented them with a silky classic fondue of Gruyère and Emmentaler. The point is to offer a variety of delights for all the senses. If you'll present your cheeses and wines on a buffet, consider arranging them from left to right or in a circle, starting with the mildest and working in one direction toward the fuller flavors (this is the order most cheese experts would recommend, so you don't overwhelm your palate with stronger flavors before tasting the milder ones). Most good cheese shops offer descriptions of their cheeses (and the same is becoming true for wines), so if you like, you can provide a tasting notes sheet or use small cards to let guests know what aromas and flavors to expect from each offering or pairing.

- **Morbier,** a semisoft cow's-milk cheese recognizable by its black layer of wood ash in the center, is full-flavored and has a slightly bitter finish.
- **Clochette,** a bell-shaped goat cheese, is aged for one month and has a strong herbal flavor.
- **Explorateur,** a fabulous triple-crème cow's-milk cheese, boasts a rich, buttery texture.

NEXT LEVEL!

Consider turning your event into a "blind" tasting. Cover wine bottles with paper bags or, better yet, pour wines into identical carafes, each with a number. (Real wine-crazy folks can make certain assumptions just by the shape of the bottle!) Instead of labeling the cheeses, simply put a number next to each one, then give guests a list of cheese and wine names and see who can guess the identities of cheeses and wines most accurately. Maybe the winner gets a nice bottle of wine or port or a gift certificate to a gourmet cheese store.

- **Chaumes,** a cow's-milk cheese, has a soft, springy texture and mild flavor.
- **Epoisses** is a pungent, earthy, and intense cow's-milk cheese.
- **Bleu d'Auvergne,** a blue cow's-milk cheese, is creamy, tangy, and very full-flavored.
- **Gruyère and Emmentaler,** used in our fondue in equal parts, are both hard cow's-milk cheeses often combined in classic Swiss fondue recipes. Gruyère is a bit more nutty and grainy, while Emmentaler features large holes and has a sweet, mild flavor.

tip

Vary your tasting choices from mild to full-flavored cheeses, and choose wines that work well with each to create unique pairings. Offer hard and soft varieties and throw in a few unexpected selections, like those made from goat's and sheep's milk as well as the more classic cow's-milk varieties. Note that some cheeses have been aged more than others. Often, the longer a cheese is aged, the more intense its flavor.

aperitifs/drinks

Offer classic Brasserie-style aperitifs as guests arrive. Lillet Blanc and Dubonnet Rouge are wine-based spirits infused with aromatics. Served over ice with a wedge of orange and a splash of club soda, they are refreshing and wonderful.

wines

We chose a range of simple French wines for this tasting, and most of our bottles were priced at under fifteen dollars each.

music

Layer your party atmosphere with sounds from the same region as the cheeses and wines you're serving. For this tasting, focus on a mix of French artists, classic and current.

RECOMMENDED ARTISTS:

- Edith Piaf, *The Voice of the Sparrow*
- Claude Bolling, *Bolling's Greatest Hits* and *Paris Swing*
- Django Reinhardt, *The Indispensable Django Reinhardt* (Jazz Tribute #39)
- Vanessa Paradis, *Bliss*

décor

Arrange cheese boards (or cutting boards) and pretty platters, keeping stronger cheeses separate from their milder counterparts. There are lots of beautiful cheese accessories and special knives and

PAIR BUBBLY WITH CREAMY CHEESES

Sparkling wine happens to be a wonderful match for creamy cheeses like Brie and Saint André. Although true Champagne is made only in the Champagne region of France, there are wonderful, less-expensive sparkling French wines, such as Crémant d'Alsace. Ask your wine shop adviser or check out one of the many helpful wine websites on the Internet (see Resources, page 200, for more information).

spreaders available, but if you don't have them, don't worry—just make sure each cheese has its own knife to avoid mixing flavors.

Drape sultry grapes here and there and use beautiful breads to accent your display. Don't worry about matching glassware—mixing up wineglasses is fine and can make it easier for folks to identify their glasses as they move from pairing to pairing.

If you're serious about the tasting process, resist the temptation to decorate with fragrant flowers or scented candles—their strong aromas can affect your ability to smell and taste accurately.

di-vine detail

Show off the latest oeno-gadget. It's a wineglass holder that clips onto any standard plate, allowing guests to manage both wine and cheese with just one hand. These generally come in sets and are affordable enough to give as presents to your guests so they'll have them for future tastings.

holiday toast

There's just something about the holidays. Although they're busy and bustling, I always want to take the time to get together with friends, coworkers, and family to celebrate one of the most festive times of the year. My sister Sara is really the queen of the holidays in our clan—every year she hosts a White Elephant Holiday Party where we all exchange funny, inexpensive gifts like DVDs of silly movies, action figures, and microwaveable cat-shaped aromatherapy neck pillows (that was one of my offerings).

Sara whips up fantastic baked dips and yummy meatballs, and my brother David mixes the cocktails. The best part is, I don't have to do anything except show up in something sparkly and drink Prosecco! And every year, certain goofy gifts, like bacon-shaped bandages and a Rocky weight belt, make their reappearance.

With or without the white elephant component, this party is sure to make your guests sparkle and smile. I've presented lush dishes in smaller, cocktail-style sizes, and I've narrowed drink choices to make planning the party easy. Of course, you can add a winter lager or your favorite spiced wine, but if you just offer wine or Champagne, consider marking guests' glasses with colorful mini-bows to avoid mix-ups.

the menu

- Mini Smoked Salmon Sandwiches
- Shrimp & Crab Bisque with Parmesan Croutons
- Baby Lamb Chops with Goat Cheese & Herbs
- Gingersnaps, fine chocolates, and petits fours (ours are from Payard Patisserie)
- Amaretto Hot Chocolate

apertifs/drinks

Sazeracs and Rudolph Fizzes

wines

Keep it simple and sparkly—serve bubbly only! Champagne is the more luxe choice, while cava or Prosecco are more economical yet still fabulously festive. If you like, you could add a dessert wine to pair with the cookies and sweets.

music

Mix up traditional favorites with new holiday twists for a warm, contemporary vibe.

RECOMMENDED ARTISTS:

- Diana Krall, *Christmas Songs*
- *Celtic Christmas: A Windham Hill Sampler*
- George Winston, *December*
- *This Christmas: Songs from the Motion Picture*
- Josh Groban, *Noel*
- Harry Connick, Jr., *Harry for the Holidays*

hint

Transforming these cocktail party favorites into satisfying dinner fare is incredibly easy—and it's all in the presentation. Just serve the Mini Smoked Salmon Sandwiches or another choice from the Small Bites section (page 119) when guests arrive. At the table, offer the Shrimp & Crab Bisque in soup bowls as an appetizer, and allow four baby lamb chops per guest for your main course. If you like, add a simple green salad, or whip up a batch of Creamed Spinach Royale or Truffled Mashed Potatoes (page 158) to accompany them.

décor

Choose a fresh, winter-inspired color theme for your party, with snowy white as a base color and decorative accents of glimmering silver and glossy red. If you prefer cooler colors, turquoise or cobalt blue would make a wonderful alternative to the bright red details. Present your refreshments on a table in a central location. Move chairs away from the table so that guests can access food and drinks on all sides or set up a bar at one end of the space to avoid crowding.

If you'll trim a tree at the party, create a make-your-own ornament station, with simple glass balls in silver, white, and red. Set out colorful markers, glue sticks, and decorative glitter. If kids will be there, add stickers and let them take their creations home at the end of the party. You could apply this same principle to a holiday card station for the kids—provide them with colorful paper instead of ornaments and let them create their own unique season's greetings!

Use mirror tiles (available at home stores) to form a pattern or line them up to create a runner on your table. The reflection picks up candlelight nicely and adds a bit of extra shimmer (and the illusion of more space) to your room. I filled glass cylinders with inexpensive, colorful ornaments (you could substitute apples or adorn the cylinders with gift wrap or ribbon) and placed platters on top to create a multitiered display.

merry cherry detail

Because of the time of year, you might want to create a party favor to give to your guests. I suggest my homemade Cherry Syrup (page 114), which takes just minutes to make and can be packaged in pretty bottles. When kept in the refrigerator, this versatile syrup will last for months and can be used on pancakes, in drinks, and over ice cream or cake.

NEXT LEVEL!

Add some extra warmth to your party (and your community) by inviting each of your guests to bring an unwrapped new toy or book. In a corner, set up a gift-wrap station with fun papers and ribbon, and let guests (and their kids) wrap the presents during the party. At the end, collect all the wrapped gifts and drop them at a local shelter or church group. Talk about holiday cheer!

I love the word *supper.* It's so cozy and inviting. For me it evokes images of folks eating tasty, satisfying food, telling stories, and laughing out loud. Its friendly format is ideal for a family-style meal on a Sunday night, a girls' get-together, or a feisty game night celebration, all of which you'll find in these pages. • The forgiving nature of a supper allows for the

casual suppers

melding of various cuisines and the dropping by of friends throughout the evening. And yet, with a few simple, creative touches, you can make your supper sing and transform it into a party that is super laid-back, but oh-so stylish! • When you're ready to eat, you can take your meal at the table, or on the couch, or sitting on the floor. Why? Because it's relaxed and easy. It's supper, and that's worth celebrating.

zen ladies' night

This wonderful evening starts with a workshop-themed welcome, designed to help busy ladies relax, take a deep breath, and de-stress.

The idea here is to hire a personal trainer, dance teacher, or yoga instructor to come to your place early in the evening for an hour-long group workshop designed to make you all feel great. Focus the hour on techniques for de-stressing and relaxing or just having fun. After stretching, meditating, or moving to the music, you all gather round for delicious cocktails and a healthful supper.

Keep your menu nutritious yet sumptuous—serve Red Miso–baked Salmon with Scallions and Asian Noodle Salad with Peanut Dressing, both of which are incredibly easy to prepare and can be made in advance. Dessert might be scoops of green tea or vanilla ice cream with cookies and hot tea.

the menu

- Preworkshop pick-me-up: granola or cereal bars
- Red Miso–baked Salmon with Scallions
- Baby Arugula Salad with Grapefruit & Avocado
- Asian Noodle Salad with Peanut Dressing
- Green tea ice cream (store bought)

aperitifs/drinks

Before the workshop, offer sparkling water with a splash of juice, or serve hot green tea. Afterward, offer the ladies refreshing Pomegranate Cherry Sakejitos or Plum Wine Spritzers.

wines

Light wines with crisp acidity and herbal, floral, or spicy notes—for example, Sauvignon Blanc, Riesling, or Vouvray.

décor

Decorate with natural colors and materials in a soft, neutral palette. Use an Asian-style rubber stamp to personalize napkin rings. Accent your dining table with a hint of color—pretty chopsticks in pink, for example. Fill ceramic or wood bowls with floating flowers and candles to add a spa-like feeling.

tip

PUTTING YOUR WORKSHOP TOGETHER

Hiring an instructor doesn't have to be expensive, if you all chip in. Or, as the host, you could pick up the tab for the workshop and ask each guest to bring a dish or a bottle of wine or sake.

music

Choose from the wide variety of what some call "soundscapes"—new-agey tunes that are both stimulating and relaxing, featuring electronica and nature sounds along with groovy beats. A laid-back loungelike vibe works well too.

RECOMMENDED ARTISTS:

- *Café Chillout: Costa del Mar Lounge Ibiza* (various artists)
- *New Age Masters: Mystery to Revelation* (various artists)
- Thievery Corporation, *The Mirror Conspiracy*
- *Buddha-Bar Nature* (various artists)
- Kate Bush, *The Sensual World*
- Norah Jones, Sade, or other soft jazz and R&B

tip

I created this party with a Zen-inspired theme, focusing on a relaxing workshop and a mellow dinner party filled with healthful, light foods. But if you'd like to rev up your ladies' night festivities, you could start with an hour-long salsa workshop (taught by a hot instructor!), followed—or accompanied—by the Latin Spice Cocktail party menu of food and drinks (page 44). Yet another idea: a belly dancing workshop followed by a Global Potluck supper (page 66).

THE GIFT OF PAMPERING

If you have the time and the inclination, why not create wonderful homemade body scrubs for your girlfriends to take home? See page 114 for the how-to.

serene details

Make sure there is plenty of space for your workshop, ideally in a room or area separate from your dining space. If it's a beautiful evening, host this part outside under the big sky in your backyard or at a nearby park, then head inside to share a meal.

As a special touch, I was able to find cheap, cute straw mats to use for the workshop. I got them at one of my favorite New York City stores, Pearl River, an incredible Chinese department store (which also has a website for online shopping—see Resources). It's one of my go-to party resources for well-designed, cheap goods, from clothing and accessories to papers, plates, and Asian foods. I used good-luck rubber stamp characters to create gift cards for the mats, and gave away little journals, pink chopsticks, and chopstick holders for less than ten dollars per person, making me look incredibly stylish and generous!

Burn incense and candles throughout your home—opt for light, refreshing citrus-based scents rather than heavy, musky fragrances.

global potluck

For this party, I've taken inspiration from the exotic flavors and textures of North Africa and South Asia, but you can choose any regions that suit your taste. It's fun to assign each guest a place—Casablanca, Cairo, Mumbai (Bombay)—and maybe include a hint about what element to bring (beverage, appetizer, main course, or dessert). You could communicate this via email or, if you want to get a bit more ambitious, send a postcard with a picture or map of their assigned place and a suggested dish. Then get ready for an evening of festive flavors.

the menu

Of course your guests will be bringing delicious dishes to share, but if you'd like to supplement with a few wonderful treats, consider these ideas.

- Baby Lamb Chops with Goat Cheese & Herbs
- Coconut Chicken Curry
- Parsley Couscous
- Cucumber Raita with Dill, served with store-bought naan bread
- Stewed Okra, Peas & Tomatoes
- Store-bought Indian sweets

aperitifs/drinks

Tunisian Mint Tea, Pomegranate Cherry Sakejitos, Plum Wine Spritzers, or Grand Margaritas. Also consider serving one of India's fantastic and refreshing beers, such as Taj Mahal (in big bottles) or Kingfisher.

wines

Spicy, floral Rieslings and Gewürtztraminers make wonderful white wine matches with the bold flavors of Africa and India as do fruity rosés and light red wines.

music

Indian "Bollywood" movies are full of song and dance, as well as beautiful costumes and dramatic escapades. Why not play one in the background during dinner? Look for anything featuring my favorite leading man, Shahrukh Khan. There are also lots of good compilations featuring music styles from all over the world. Search for "world music" on any music website and download a gorgeous tapestry of sounds for your party.

RECOMMENDED ARTISTS:

- Anything by Sukhwinder Singh
- *Bollywood Boxset* (various artists)
- *Buddha World Lounge: Ethno Chillout Bar* (various artists)
- Jeli Moussa Sissoko, *Kora Music from Mali*

décor

Set your potluck supper out as a buffet and serve everything out of attractive pots and pans arranged on a countertop or on your dining table. Use boldly colored runners or place mats (or even ceramic tiles or foreign newspapers) as a backdrop for the food. We used a rubber stamp to create passport-inspired cards to identify guests' culinary creations.

Buy a few inexpensive paper lanterns and display them along with lots of glowing votive candles. Toss some pretty throw pillows here and there and let folks gather around a low coffee table or on couches and ottomans. Burn incense in your bathroom or at the entrance to your home. Serve wine and tea in small Moroccan glasses.

tip

EASY EXOTIC ACCENT

In a decorative pinch? Just break off the petals from half a dozen flowers (look for marigolds or carnations, which are often used in India, or substitute rose petals) in bright colors—red, hot pink, orange—and scatter them along the center of your dining table, clustering votive candles or lanterns to add a soft glow.

game night get-together

SCORE A BIG WIN WITH YOUR FAVORITE SPORTS FANS

GO TEAM!

This super supper is not only perfect for any game day or night at home—the easy dishes and ideas are perfect for you tailgaters out there, too. My World's Best Chili might even become your MVPF (most valuable party food). My friends ask for it all the time!

Game night requires sofa-friendly munchies that are hearty and satisfying, fun and casual. No need to reinvent the wheel here—we've simply taken some classic game night foods and given them a fresh twist or two. The best part is, everything here can be made in advance and put together quickly just before guests arrive. Add a few clever details and get ready to kick off the festivities.

the menu

- Hot Wings with Pineapple Glaze & Creamy Blue Cheese Dip
- Sweet & Spicy Parmesan Popcorn
- Baby Romaine Salad with Corn, Cucumber & Cilantro Vinaigrette
- World's Best Chili
- Go Team Cupcakes

aperitifs/drinks

Dark & Stormys, old-fashioned root beer in bottles or mugs, and microbrewed beer from your favorite team's home state or city.

wines

Young, spicy red wines will pair well with the chili and the wings. Try a peppery Tempranillo from Spain or a juicy Shiraz from Australia or New Zealand.

music

Anything that gets you fired up for the big showdown! Whether it's classic rock, cool country, or awesome

NEXT LEVEL!

Create a Quick Team Trivia Challenge. During a commercial break, ask five to ten questions about players, championships, and statistics. (If you don't have time to research the questions yourself, a sports-themed Trivial Pursuit card or two will work well.) You can play individually or group folks into small teams and have players write down their answers. Tally up the scores and announce the winners during the next commercial break. The prize? A sports highlights DVD, a baseball cap, or just the impressive title of Supreme Quick Team Trivia Challenge Champion of the World!

KEEP FOODS WITHIN EASY REACH

Once the game gets going, you don't want to have to jump up every few minutes when someone needs something. We arranged our game night foods on a big coffee table, but you could set up supper on a folding card table with a team-colored tablecloth thrown over the top. You can also pack this whole party to go and enjoy it tailgate-style.

tip

eighties music, get it going early because you'll have to turn it down once the action starts!

RECOMMENDED ARTISTS:
Anything by Bon Jovi, Garth Brooks, Queen, or Kiss, or an eighties hair band or dance compilation.

décor

Decorate in your team's official colors. Order inexpensive custom napkins and coasters online (ours are from www.foryourparty.com) and personalize them with your favorite slogans. Make an easy centerpiece out of wheatgrass from your local farmers' market or garden center. Just add a football, tennis balls, or your sports props of choice and—voilà!—instant atmosphere. Wear your favorite jersey and write "[Their Team] Sucks!" in erasable marker on your bathroom mirror (filling in the opposing team's name). Personalize your Go Team Cupcakes with little flags bearing victory cries or players' names.

"Having friends over for dinner" sounds fun, easy, and relaxing. "Hosting a dinner party" sounds serious, time-consuming, and possibly scary. Do you have to find a special occasion? Must you dress up and serve your guests a multicourse meal? • The answer to all of the above is, only if you want to. Personally, I love a dinner party precisely because it offers a chance to celebrate at home with a little extra panache. After

all, there are times when you're excited to plan a fancier menu, set a formal table, and even knock some socks off with your entertaining style! • So while a dinner party doesn't require a special occasion, the parties in this section will hopefully inspire one! To create them, I took inspiration from the seasons—one to celebrate the fresh herbs of summer, one for cozy autumn holidays, and one for New Year's Eve, because I prefer to stay close to home on this big night, but I still like a little sparkle.

herbal essences

This party is a true foodie's fantasy. It's designed to celebrate fresh herbs, and even though most herbs are now available fresh throughout the year, to me this is a warm-weather dinner with an emphasis on lighter fare. Filled with layers of bright flavors, aromas, and colors, this is one dinner party that looks good, smells great, and tastes even better.

We hosted this party in a loftlike apartment with a fabulous view of Manhattan, but it would be perfect as an *al fresco* dinner on a patio, terrace, or back lawn as well.

The feeling of this whole evening should be fresh and natural. I added a colorful palette of lavenders and greens to punch up the mood. I also let myself be inspired by fresh herbs in all areas of the celebration, including a special cocktail and the table decorations, which can provide a gift for each guest.

Mary's Lavender Panna Cotta, my favorite recipe for this party, is named after its creator, my friend Chef Mary Cleaver. It's surprisingly easy to make and so fragrant and creamy! Serve it with a sweet Tokay Pinot Gris dessert wine or a glass of Tunisian Mint Tea (page 197).

NEXT LEVEL!

Warm weather in New York City brings out the best in our farmers' markets. (Can you believe we have farmers' markets in the middle of New York City?) I love to shop there for locally grown foods whenever I can, especially for a party like this, where most of the ingredients are very simply prepared. Their freshness really shines through.

the menu

- Cucumber Raita with Dill
  (served with crunchy vegetables)
- Cavatappi Salad with Peas, Ricotta, Basil & Mint
- Oven-roasted Halibut with Cherry Tomatoes & Thyme
- Baby Potato Salad with Oregano
- Mary's Lavender Panna Cotta

aperitifs/drinks

Lemon Verbena Vodka Coolers, Malik's Tropical Rosé Sangria, Pomegranate Cherry Sakejitos, or White Wine Spritzers

wines

I recommend a good crisp Sauvignon Blanc, since it's a grape known for its herbaceous aromas and flavors, but a floral Riesling or Gewürtztraminer or even a light-style Chardonnay would be lovely as well.

music

Keep the mood mellow and relaxed, with soft jazz or other breezy tunes.

RECOMMENDED ARTISTS:

- Incognito, *Best of Incognito*
- Steve Winwood, *Nine Lives*
- Michael Franks, *Blue Pacific*
- Pat Metheny, *One Quiet Night*
- Seals & Crofts, *Greatest Hits*
- Dave Brubeck, *The Essential Dave Brubeck*

décor

Fill small pots with miniature herb plants (I got mine at the greenmarket, but you can find them at garden centers as well). Place one at each guest's setting with his or her name written on the pot or a garden stake. Choose a color theme that complements the green of the herbs—my table was inspired by a vibrant striped-purple place mat that also tied in with the Mary's Lavender Panna Cotta, but bright reds and yellows (think cherry tomatoes) would work well too. Line candles along counters and windowsills and add a scented candle with an herbal aroma to your foyer or powder room.

menu card detail

If you'd like to acquaint guests with the flavors they'll be experiencing, you might consider printing a menu card on your home computer. If your party is small enough, you could even create a menu by writing on a long, flat green leaf. Ti leaves would be good for this project, as they are smooth, come in solid green, and are available at most florist shops. You'll need a permanent paint pen or marker (I recommend white ink), which you'll find at your local arts and crafts store. The leaves will vary a bit in shape and size, which will make a lovely, organic visual touch on your tabletop. When you're ready to write, start near the tip of the leaf and work your way

GIVE THE GIFT OF AROMATHERAPY

As an alternative to the mini potted herb gifts, you could give each guest a take-home favor of Sugar Body Scrub with Lavender (see page 114).

down line by line toward the stem—or get creative. If you prefer a more uniform look, cut off the top and bottom of each leaf to make leaf rectangles. Scatter the menu leaves at each guest's setting, or tuck the leaf rectangles into the pockets of folded napkins for a polished presentation.

comfort harvest

Although I haven't mentioned it in the title, and there's no turkey involved, this might just be my ultimate Thanksgiving dinner. I love the fact that everyone gets their own whole bird (and two drumsticks each!) and of course with the cooking time of the hens being just over an hour, it's a practical (and delicious) alternative to the big T.

So even though I consider this the perfect holiday feast, it's also a menu fit for a dinner party on any autumn night. Whether you make every single recipe here or offer a smaller selection of dishes, you'll be grateful for any leftovers, because they all just get better the next day! Speaking of which, a number of these recipes can be made a day or two in advance. I've noted this for you in the recipe section.

For the menu, I've highlighted the best of what the harvest has to offer, and as always, I recommend shopping for organic products whenever possible. If you have access to a greenmarket, autumn can be a wonderful time to buy local pears, apples, and potatoes. If not, make the most of what you have available.

I'm pretty sure someone famous said something about gratitude being the key to happiness, and I happen to agree. If you like the notion of

sharing an attitude of gratitude with your guests, I've come up with a few fun ways to do so, including a napkin ring idea and a bucket of thankful thoughts to be passed around. There's such magic in that moment when folks are gathered together at the table and someone reads or shares something with the group—it's truly food for thought!

the menu

- Crab & Shrimp Bisque with Parmesan Croutons
- Roasted Maple-glazed Cornish Game Hens
- Classic Herb Stuffing
- Cranberry Clementine Sauce
- Truffled Mashed Potatoes
- Brussels Sprouts with Bacon & Balsamic
- Pear Apple Crisp

aperitifs/drinks

Offer classic, bubbly Kir Royales when your guests arrive. Later, serve a mellow Calvados (a rustic French apple brandy) with the Pear Apple Crisp.

wines

With the bisque, an unoaked California Chardonnay or a crisp Pinot Blanc would be a good choice. The soft, supple fruit of a Pinot Noir from France, Oregon, or Washington State would work beautifully with the Cornish hens and the earthy side dishes.

music

Create a cozy backdrop to this comforting feast with a low-key, offbeat shuffle of folk, alternative, and acoustic sounds.

RECOMMENDED ARTISTS:

- Acoustic Alchemy, *The New Edge*
- Al Di Meola, *Elegant Gypsy*
- Nick Drake, *Pink Moon* or *Way to Blue*
- Anything by Celtic Fiddle Festival
- Damien Rice, *Live from the Union Chapel*
- *Sun Chasers: Native American Flute Works* (various artists)

décor

Reds and oranges are classic autumn hues, but why not choose a fresh color palette? We used a combination of blue, white, and green to bring a bit of lightness to an otherwise rich, dark setting. Combine your most elegant table settings with rustic kitchen towel place mats in varying patterns to create an eclectic, warm feeling. As an alternative to pumpkins and leaves, decorate with a centerpiece of bright-green Granny Smith apples in an heirloom-style bowl or compote. I like to add a few different types of candles as well—lanterns and votives—so there is glowing light on several levels.

earthy detail

Want pretty place cards for your formal table? Look in your refrigerator. Button mushrooms make sweet, seasonal name card holders. Choose 'shrooms that

NEXT LEVEL!

GIVING THANKS TOGETHER

Print out quotes about gratitude by your favorite writers, artists, poets, and thinkers. Fold them and put them in a basket or pail to be passed around the dinner table. Each person takes a quote and reads it aloud to the group, sparking conversation and filling the moment with the spirit of shared thankfulness.

For another twist on this idea, I've also made napkin rings out of my thankful quotes. It's easy. Just print out the quotes on strips of paper or card stock (recycled brown paper or mix-and-match paper remnants would be great for this project). Set your margins to at least two inches on each side. Type your guest's name and a thoughtful quote in the center section of the paper, then wrap the paper around the napkin to make a band.

will stand up on their heads. Cut a slit in the end of the woody stem and insert a small (two by three inches or so) card lettered with a guest's name. Set a card at each place setting and you have an accent that is unique, personal, inexpensive, and ecofriendly.

new year's eve
steakhouse-style

Personally, I never like to go out on New Year's Eve. Maybe it's all those years I spent in restaurants working till four in the morning and sweeping up confetti. Or maybe it's my sense that there's just more value to be had on this most expensive night by purchasing great ingredients, spending a little time in the kitchen, and inviting friends to bring themselves (and a bottle of bubbly) for an intimate celebration of the time that's passing and the possibilities ahead.

If you like, you can pull out all the stops at your New Year's Eve fête. It's a great occasion for breaking out all your best china, splurging on a special Champagne, and wearing something sparkly! I've put together this party with simple preparations of high-end ingredients such as foie gras and caviar, but of course you can omit those optional elements, or even substitute dishes from other parties in the book. For example, it would be easy and economical to replace the beef fillet with the baby lamb chops recipe on page 123. And the smoked salmon sandwiches from the Holiday Toast cocktail gathering (recipe on page 120) would make a wonderful alternative to the scallop amuse-bouche.

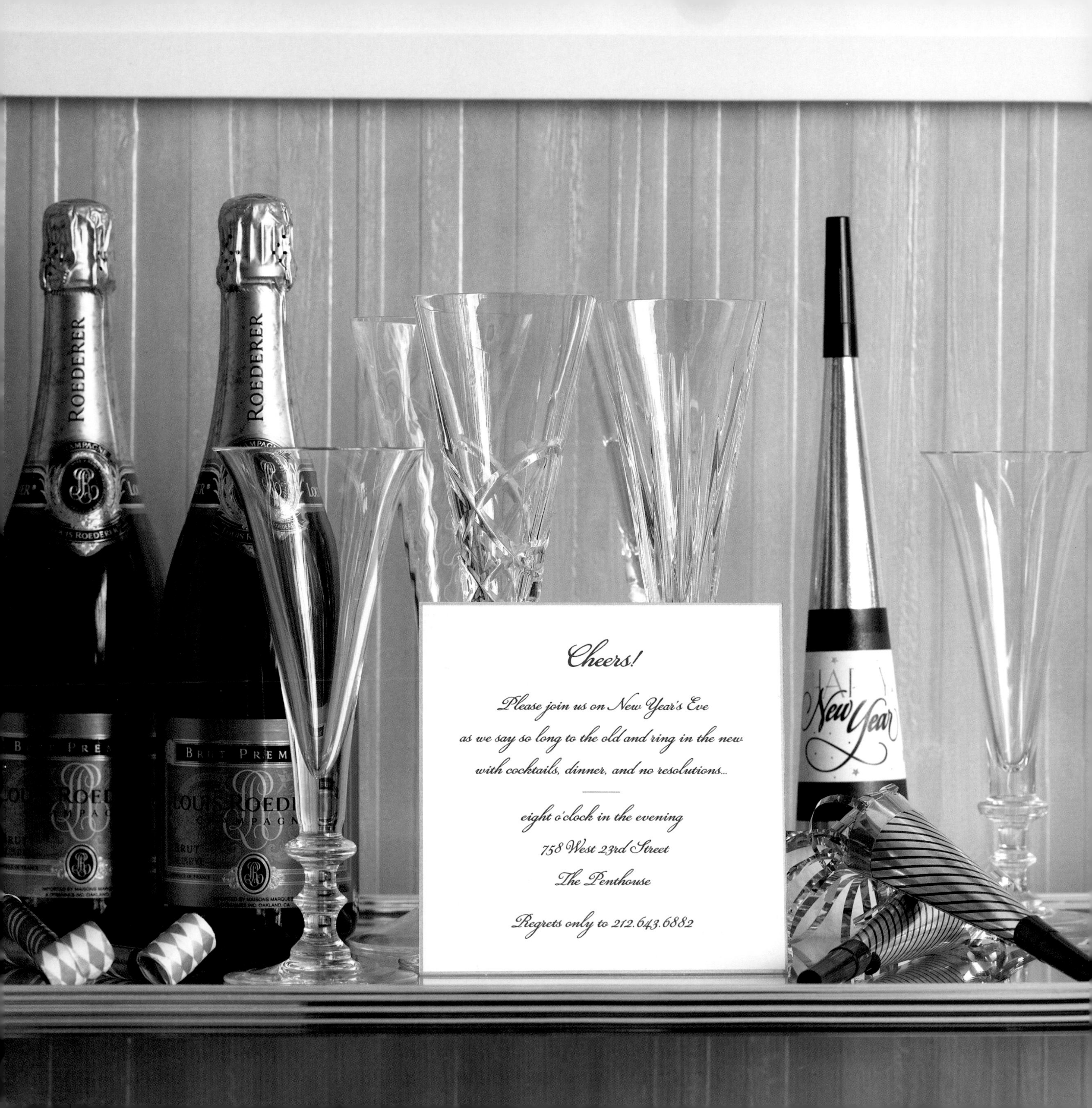

ROEDERER
ROEDERER
Cheers!
Please join us on New Year's Eve
as we say so long to the old and ring in the new
with cocktails, dinner, and no resolutions...
eight o'clock in the evening
758 West 23rd Street
The Penthouse
Regrets only to 212.643.6882
New Year

the menu

- Scallop & Caviar Amuse-bouche
- White Lasagna with Wild Mushrooms
- Seared Fillet of Beef with Foie Gras Chapeau & Balsamic Pan Sauce
- Creamed Spinach Royale
- Truffled Mashed Potatoes
- Ice Cream with Amaretto & Chocolate Abstracts

aperitifs/drinks

Classic Vodka Martinis and Kir Royales

wines

Serve Champagne with the scallops and the lasagna (try a rosé Champagne for a fresh twist), then move to a big red wine for the main course. Barolo, the Italian giant with hints of tobacco and tar, would be a perfect choice, as would a classic Bordeaux blend or a powerful Spanish Rioja.

music

Start off the evening with a festive retro vibe for cocktails and dinner, then kick up the energy a few notches as the clock ticks ever closer to next year!

RECOMMENDED ARTISTS:

- Michael Bublé, *Call Me Irresponsible*
- Dean Martin, *Dino: The Essential Dean Martin*
- *The Ultimate Diva Collection* (various artists)
- Anything by Prince or Michael Jackson and all your favorite eighties tunes
- Destiny's Child, *#1's*
- *Def Jam Recordings: Let the People Speak* (various artists)

MAKE THESE RECIPES AHEAD

The White Lasagna can be prepared and baked up to two days in advance, and the Creamed Spinach Royale and Chocolate Abstracts can each be made one day before the party. Just reheat the lasagna (I suggest adding a few pats of butter on top before putting it in the oven) and the spinach when you're ready. Take the frozen chocolate pieces out after you've scooped the ice cream into the glasses.

décor

This party was set in a gorgeous apartment designed by Campion Platt at New York City's famed Manhattan House. Here, I opted for an elegant palette of black and white, accented by metallics in silver and gold. You can add a special glass to your place setting, as we did with our black Champagne flutes. They make a striking complement to the marble table and the other crystal stemware.

I created a "black-tie" napkin ring from satin ribbon, and tucked in a festive noisemaker as a party favor. The centerpiece is all about light. I arranged a group of gold taper candles, tucked into a mix of fancy crystal and inexpensive glass candlesticks. I added gold glass votives for even more glow. Party hats give the setting a super-festive feeling as the old year winds down and the new one winds up!

dinner interactive

Instead of making resolutions, celebrate saying goodbye to the old and hello to the new. Place two vessels on your dinner table (use glass vases, silver bowls, or gold urns). Make a sign or label for one vessel that says "Out with the OLD" and another that reads "In with the NEW." Set out blank slips of paper at each guest's place and encourage folks to write down what's "out" for their new year and what's "in," placing their folded notes in either the "in" or "out" bowls. Then, during dinner, have guests take turns reading from the slips of paper and enjoy talking, laughing, and being inspired!

There's just something about starting a party in the late morning or afternoon. It seems as though the fun will last forever. All the parties in this section are inspired by my family and friends. As I mentioned, my sister Sara hosts a White-Elephant Cocktail Party every Christmas, so I took her idea and turned it into a Regift Exchange Brunch, where folks swap items they

a brunch, a lunch & a linner

don't use. • The panini picnic tradition began when I won my first panini maker at a silent auction. I became obsessed with these rustic sandwiches and all their endless variations. I would truly have a picnic every day if the weather (and my job) permitted. • And the barbecue? Well, let's just say I imagine heaven as a place where the all-you-can-eat buffet includes saucy ribs and the frozen margarita fountain is open very, very late.

regift exchange brunch

OLD IS NEW AGAIN AT THIS WHITE-ELEPHANT KITCHEN EXCHANGE

I do love brunch, don't you? It's a kick-back meal where you get to eat like a kid and at the same time are authorized to drink Champagne in the middle of the day.

I also love presents, so I took my sister Sara's idea of a white-elephant gift exchange theme to a new, environmentally friendly place with this party. Guests choose an object they own but don't want anymore and wrap it as a gift. I chose a theme of kitchen gadgets, but you could make it anything you like—summer clothes, costume jewelry, tableware—you name it!

Each gift bag is marked with a number corresponding to numbered, folded slips of paper placed in a bowl or box. One at a time, each guest draws a number, then claims and opens the gift. As the gift opening proceeds, the person who has just claimed a gift can "steal" from anyone who's already opened something, if they want to. In the end, you have a fun activity, a great meal, and a spirit of recycling in this "everything old is new again" approach to a weekend afternoon.

the menu

- Stuffed Brioche French Toast with Mascarpone & Chocolate
- Seasonal Fruit Salad with Fresh Mint
- Potato, Sausage & Gruyère Gratin

aperitifs/drinks

French Peach Brunch Punch, White Wine Spritzers, Amaretto Hot Chocolate

wines

Bubbly, of course—a cava from Spain, a slightly sweet Asti from Italy, or a classic Champagne

music

Keep it quiet and sweet, with shades of classical and vintage favorites and alternative soft rock.

RECOMMENDED ARTISTS:

- Ingrid Michaelson, *Slow the Rain*
- Karl Wolff, *Classical Music for Guitar*
- Josephine Baker, *J'ai Deux Amours*
- Ahn Trio, *Lullaby for My Favorite Insomniac*
- Doris Day, *The Complete Standard Transcriptions*

décor

You can host this party in any kind of environment, modern or traditional, classic or eclectic. Our setting was a whimsical apartment designed by the

incredible Maureen Footer, so we opted for a fantasy mix-and-match vintage-inspired table setting, incorporating pieces from Reynaud, Bernardaud, and Versace. We accented this luxurious table with simple, sunny details. Our floral arrangements were made from daffodils bought at a local grocery store and packed into Versace's fabulous butterfly-themed coffee and tea pourers. You could also work with the "green" theme for this brunch, setting your table with mismatched plates, glasses, and teacups from the flea market.

panini picnic

You can turn a picnic into a potluck, asking every-one to bring something, or you can pack everything you need in one of the great picnic backpacks or rolling bags that are available these days. Some of them come with plates, wineglasses, silverware, even wine openers and napkins!

the menu

- Focaccia Panini with Prosciutto à la Caprese
- Baby Potato Salad with Oregano
- Radicchio & Carrot Slaw
- Haricots Verts with Lemon & Parmesan
- Lady fingers with Amaretto or Vin Santo

hint

If you have room, throw a fluffy pillow or two into a tote bag for extra comfort. I also like to bring a plastic drop cloth (available at most hardware stores) to lay underneath my picnic blanket. It helps keep the blanket (and my clothes) dry and stain-free.

aperitifs/drinks

Look for Italian citrus sodas, like Limonata and Aranciata—they are refreshing and crisp, as are my favorite Italian beers, Moretti and Peroni. Take along extra bottled water if you'll be walking a lot.

wines

Before you leave the house, chill a bottle of Dolcetto d'Alba, a simple, fruity, and light red wine from the Piedmont region of Italy. Or bring Brachetto d'Acqui, a bubbly Italian red wine, which has a little sweetness. A crisp Pinot Grigio or Prosecco would also do nicely on a sunny afternoon!

music

If you're picnicking in a park or away from home, chances are, you'll be happy to enjoy the natural music of the birds, trees, or water surrounding you. If you're on the patio or terrace (or your living-room floor), perhaps you'd like a little Italian flavor with your *buon gusto*?

RECOMMENDED ARTISTS:

- Toto Cutugno, *L'Italiano*
- Mina, *L'immensità*
- Umberto Tozzi, *The Best of Umberto Tozzi*
- Zucchero, *All the Best*

AMARETTO OR VIN SANTO?

Amaretto is an almond-flavored liqueur from Italy. It's earthy and spirited, and as you'll note by the number of recipes in which I include it, I like it! Vin Santo is another great option. It is a dessert wine made from grapes that are harvested very late and then dried on straw mats to intensify their flavor. It's wonderful for sipping or as a dip for biscotti or the previously mentioned lady fingers, both of which are available at most good grocery stores in the baked goods section.

décor

The great thing about a picnic is it really doesn't require much decorating—after all, someone very clever already hung that gorgeous sun in the sky and put those trees just where they belong. The setting itself, whether it's a lush park, a beautiful hill with a view, a sandy dune, or any pretty spot, will become the backdrop for your party. To create a more polished look, you can accessorize your picnic portfolio with a color-coordinated blanket, tote, and napkins, as we've done here, but the charming nature of a picnic makes it totally forgiving of these minor details in favor of just having fun. *Buon divertimento!*

green detail

If you prefer to take disposable plates and glasses, check out the ecofriendly options at verterra.com, or if you'd like to create your own permanent picnic tableau, look for lightweight acacia wood bowls and plates, like the ones we've used here. They are beautiful, reusable, and they won't break. Same is true for bamboo, but take note: you can't put either in the dishwasher!

backyard barbecue

FESTIVE DINING OUTSIDE IN SIMPLE STUNNING STYLE

I live in a high-rise apartment, so I don't have a backyard right now. Getting one (a backyard) is on my to-do list, but in the meantime, I often borrow the lovely, pastoral setting behind my brother David's house whenever I need a grill fix. David is the grill master in our family (and a great all-around cook), and he did all the grilling for the party pictured here, along with helping me tweak the recipes. In exchange, I got him a mini fire pit and some new plates for his outdoor entertaining.

We hosted this get-together for about ten friends (including my sister, her husband, and my adorable little nephew, whom you see pictured on page 92), and we set up a buffet-style meal and a self-serve drinks station with premade margaritas and iced tea, along with buckets of cold beer and old-fashioned sodas.

the menu
- Brother David's Grilled Chicken & Ribs
- Sweet & Tangy Barbecue Sauce
- Pineapple-glazed Shrimp Kebabs
- Grilled Southwestern Corn on the Cob
- Strawberry Angel-food Trifle

aperitifs/drinks
Margaritas Más Grandes, old-fashioned sodas in glass bottles, iced tea, microbrewed beers

wines

Focus mainly on the drinks mentioned, but have a bottle or two of a refreshing, inexpensive French rosé on hand (I like Tavel and Rosé d'Anjou) for any wine aficionados who might drop by.

music

Play fun, upbeat tunes from a variety of genres. Zydeco from New Orleans, great country music, and a little bit o' rock and roll sounds good to me! Or for a truly special treat, hire a local banjo duo to liven up the party.

RECOMMENDED ARTISTS:

- Johnny Cash, *The Essential Johnny Cash*
- Buckwheat Zydeco, *Waitin' for My Ya Ya*
- Clifton Chenier, *I'm Here!*
- John Hiatt, *Crossing Muddy Waters*
- Bluegrass Invasion (the McCormick brothers), *Bluegrass Invasion*
- Robert Cray, *Strong Persuader*
- Buddy Holly, *Greatest Hits*

décor

Keep the décor here simple and natural, but for a bit of visual punch, add boldly colored napkins, runners, or tablecloths to your picnic table. We used folding card tables for our drinks and food stations, and we topped them with inexpensive cotton tablecloths. Of course, you can serve the meal on disposable plates, if you like, but I chose to use

NEXT LEVEL!

If seeing who can eat the most ribs isn't enough, you can add a little extra competition to the mix. Play horseshoes or set up a scavenger hunt around the property with clues directing guests toward hidden objects. Give take-home bottles of your barbecue sauce or K's Famous Spice Rub (page 115) as prizes for the winners.

china and to add a dramatic charger plate and a river stone atop the napkin at each setting, to make the table feel really special. Add a few colorful lanterns, but avoid votives or other candles, as even a light breeze will blow them out.

endless drink detail

Look for super-size drink dispensers. We found our inexpensive ceramic ones (which came with erasable markers!) at a discount retailer. They really add to the look of the bar, and their large capacity eliminates (or reduces, depending upon your crowd) the need to make more drinks during the party. You can also find vintage apothecary jars at the flea market or antique store. You may want to prep a few pitchers and keep them in the fridge till you need to replenish the bar.

hint

OUTDOOR ENTERTAINING MUSTS

- Cover foods to keep bugs away. For bowls, I like to use pretty dishtowels or napkins, and for saucy items on platters, I place a cake stand topper or the bottom of a large plastic food storage container over the platter or plate. You can also find serving pieces with covers at your local homewares store.

- Protect your guests. If they can't get at the food, the bugs might try to dine on your friends, so I suggest keeping a bottle of insect repellent on hand. Look for nontoxic citronella and essential-oil-based repellents (or make your own at home from the many recipes available online) if you'd like to avoid harsh chemicals.

- Light the way. If your party will stretch past sunset, consider staking tiki torches in the lawn to help light the way. I like to create lanterns out of large, frosted-glass cylinder vases. Just add a little sand in the bottom of each vase, then scatter them here and there for a soft, glowing effect.

guest & host GIFTS

a homemade gift is always personal and often less expensive than store-bought options. This sugar body scrub costs a fraction of what you'd spend in a salon.

We all want to be thoughtful and gracious, to find the perfect present for a birthday honoree or the host of a dinner party or special occasion. So why don't we start the process earlier? How many times have you run into a store in a pinch to grab a gift or card (or bottle of wine in a wine-store foil bag) at the last minute? I used to be guilty of en-route duress shopping, buying gifts on my way to the party and wrapping frantically in my car, until I got tired of wasting money on yet another pair of scissors and another roll of tape when I already had the stuff at home. I decided to get organized about my gifting, and in this chapter I'll share some of my tips and tricks to help you do the same.

On the other side of giving, it's also fun to offer small favors or tokens to your guests when you're hosting the party. But I'm not the type to weave place mats out of leaves or make Be-Dazzled cell phone covers, so I've come up with suggestions for store-bought presents and inexpensive homemade projects that are both personal and practical.

CARD STOCK

Because I am not so great at remembering to pick up an anniversary or birthday card at the last minute, I buy a variety of fun cards when I see them and keep them in an accordion file with tabs marked "Birthdays," "Holidays," "Congrats," and the like. I keep postage stamps and a colorful marker in the file too, so there's no excuse for not filling them out or mailing them on time!

store-bought gifts

Keeping a few small gift items in your party pantry is a fabulous idea. Watch for unique sale items, and you'll always have something wonderful to give to a friend, coworker, or host on a moment's notice. Look for universal gifts. Here are a few to inspire you.

- **A bottle of something unexpected:** Hendrick's Gin, white Lillet (an orange-flavored French aperitif), rosé wine or Champagne, any single-malt Scotch, a flavored oil or vinegar, or citrusy Italian sodas like Limonata or Aranciata.
- **Gourmet packaged foods:** canned stuffed grape leaves, jars of wonderful olives or pickles, tins of butter cookies from Harrods of London or your favorite bakery, or a good pesto or tomato sauce.
- **Wine accessories:** openers, vacuum stoppers (to keep bottles fresh), and wineglass clips (as pictured on page 52).
- **Home enhancements:** bubble bath, soaps, kitchen towels, or small culinary gadgets.
- **Green gifts:** reusable tote bags, soy candles, natural cleaning products, bamboo platters or bowls, a small plant, or any lovely or useful object made from post-consumer waste. Check out www.greenfeet.com for some neat products and see page 115 for more great websites.

READY TO WRAP

Organize a gift wrap and card area in your home. I keep a bin with everything I need to wrap small to medium presents, with scissors, tape, and a variety of fun ribbons and tissue handy so that I can customize the gift to the occasion.

WIRED
WOVEN RIBBON
RUBAN TISSÉ ARMÉ

To:
From:

To:
From:

To:
From:

To:
From:

homemade gifts

CHERRY SYRUP

This syrup is so versatile—you can mix it with Champagne (Rudolph Fizz, page 191), add it to maple syrup, or drizzle it over ice cream or cake. See page 195 for the Cherry Syrup recipe.

QUICK KITCHEN HERB GARDEN

Makes 1 gift

Plant three small starter herb plants in a pretty 8-inch pot (use terra-cotta, copper, ceramic, or galvanized aluminum). Choose from everyday cooking herbs such as rosemary, basil, thyme, parsley, and oregano, and nestle them together in the pot. Add a few stones to the bottom of the pot if it doesn't have drainage to keep the roots from getting soggy. Mark each herb with a simple garden stake, and voilà— your favorite cook will have fragrant fresh herbs at her fingertips all season long!

SUGAR BODY SCRUB WITH LAVENDER

Makes 1 gift

Why pay high prices for products filled with chemicals and preservatives when you can make this fragrant scrub for a fraction of the cost?

1 cup sugar

¼ cup sea salt

1 tablespoon lemon juice

1 tablespoon olive oil

1 tablespoon lavender essential oil

1 teaspoon dried lavender flowers

In a bowl, combine the sugar and salt. Add the remaining ingredients and stir to incorporate. Spoon the scrub into a pretty glass jar (available at craft or kitchen stores).

K'S FAMOUS SPICE RUB

Makes 1 gift

This earthy spice mixture is perfect for chicken, lamb, and pork. Just rub it on your favorite meat before grilling or pan-frying, and enjoy the exotic aromas and flavors.

2 tablespoons cumin

1 tablespoon cinnamon

2 tablespoons garlic powder

1 tablespoon cayenne pepper

1 tablespoon salt

Combine all the ingredients in a bowl and stir. Spoon the spice mix into a small glass, plastic, or metal jar and you're ready to rub!

giving green

There are some fantastic home- and party-related websites on the Internet, including ecofriendly sources for gifts and home entertaining. Check out the beautiful designs on www.plateswithpurpose. com, an online retailer that sells plates made out of recycled glass and donates a portion of the proceeds to charity. Here are a few others to explore:

- pristineplanet.com
- thekarmamarket.com
- simmonsnaturals.com

hint

PACKING LEFTOVERS

Before your next party, buy some cute takeout Chinese food containers. Pack them up, seal with a decorative sticker (maybe with your initials on it), and send guests home happy. For a more environmentally friendly option, save your plastic takeout containers throughout the year, washing them thoroughly. Store them in your party pantry, add fun labels, and fill them with yummy leftovers at your next party.

the

recipes

I have found that if you serve foods in smaller portions at parties, people seem to enjoy them more. Put out a giant wedge of cheese or a large sandwich and folks are shy. Break up the wedge into smaller chunks or cut the sandwich into mini hors d'oeuvres–style "tea" sandwiches, and the darn things

small bites

disappear. Small bites are chic and fun and festive—not to mention less likely to spill. • All the dishes in this section are designed to be eaten in just a bite or two and to make beautiful presentations that are practical for a party. Many of them could be served in larger portions if you'd like to make them a more substantial part of your meal.

mini smoked salmon sandwiches

Makes 24 tea sandwiches

12 slices white bread, crusts removed

3 tablespoons olive oil

Salt and pepper

4 ounces cream cheese

2 tablespoons prepared horseradish

Juice of 1 lemon

3 tablespoons chopped fresh chives

6 ounces cold-smoked salmon, such as lox, thinly sliced

Preheat oven to 400°F. Line a baking sheet with foil or parchment. Brush each piece of bread with olive oil. Season with salt and pepper. Toast bread till just lightly golden (3 to 5 minutes), then remove from oven and let cool slightly.

While toasts are cooling, combine cream cheese, horseradish, lemon juice, and chives in the bowl of a food processor. Pulse lightly to blend.

Spread cream cheese mixture on each piece of toast. Top half the toasts with a small slice of smoked salmon. Use the other toasts to finish the sandwiches. Cut the sandwiches into quarters and serve at room temperature.

scallop & caviar amuse-bouche

Serves 6

This dish features small bay scallops, which are tender and tasty, but you could substitute one or two medium-sized scallops per person for these tiny ones. More importantly, although caviar is an optional luxury ingredient, if you choose to use it, I encourage you to buy the American farm-raised sturgeon varieties, as the wild sturgeon is in danger of extinction due to overfishing. The good news is that farm-raised caviar is less expensive but just as tasty, and there are a few great farms in the States, mainly in California. Try the ecofriendly www.sterlingcaviar.com.

2 tablespoons butter

About ¾ pound small bay scallops (allow 5 per person)

Salt and pepper

1 lemon, halved

1 tablespoon crème fraîche

2 teaspoons American sturgeon or Sevruga caviar

Melt the butter in a large skillet. Sear the scallops over high heat, about 1 minute on each side. Remove from heat and allow to cool.

Place 5 scallops in each small serving dish, season with salt and pepper, and squeeze lemon over each. Garnish each dish with a dollop of crème fraîche and a spoonful of caviar.

baby lamb chops with goat cheese & herbs

Serves 8–12 as an hors d'oeuvre, or 4 as an entrée

Party or no party, I probably make these lamb chops at home at least once every two weeks. They are so good over a salad of baby arugula (I pour the pan juices right over the lettuce) or with Parsley Couscous (page 167). They're perfect as hearty hors d'oeuvres when you're not serving a big dinner, and they make a wonderful main course if you allow three to four chops per person.

2 sprigs fresh rosemary

2 sprigs fresh thyme

½ cup soy sauce

¼ cup balsamic vinegar

2 cloves garlic, finely chopped

12 baby lamb chops, 3–4 ounces each

Pepper

One 8-ounce log fresh goat cheese,
     cold for easier slicing

Preheat oven to 425°F. Finely chop the rosemary and the thyme and combine. Set aside.

In a bowl, mix the soy sauce, balsamic vinegar, and garlic. Arrange lamb chops on a foil-lined baking dish with deep sides. Season the lamb with pepper (no salt is necessary because of the soy sauce), then pour the soy sauce mixture over the meat.

Slice the goat cheese log into 12 rounds and place one round atop each lamb chop. Sprinkle the herb mixture over the cheese.

Roast the chops for approximately 15 minutes, then broil them for a minute or two until the cheese takes on a golden color. Serve warm or at room temperature.

coconut shrimp ceviche

Makes 16 bite-sized "spoon" hors d'oeuvres or
4 appetizer portions

Traditional ceviche is made from raw seafood that is "cooked" by the citric acid in lime and grapefruit juice. I've suggested cooked shrimp for this recipe in case you're pressed for time, but you can use raw shrimp if you prefer. I suggest canned grapefruit because any skin ruins the texture of the ceviche.

¾ pound shrimp, peeled, cooked, and chilled

½ cup lime juice

½ cup canned grapefruit sections, cut into
  quarters

¼ cup coconut milk

¼ cup finely diced pickled jalapeños

2 tablespoons chopped fresh cilantro

Salt and pepper

Chop the shrimp into small pieces. In a bowl, combine the shrimp, lime juice, and grapefruit. If using raw shrimp, marinate for 40 minutes before adding the rest of the ingredients. Add the coconut milk and jalapeños and toss together. Stir in 1 tablespoon of the cilantro. Allow the mixture to marinate for 30 minutes in the refrigerator, then season with salt and pepper. Serve on Chinese soup spoons or regular tablespoons, garnished with the remaining cilantro leaves.

ciliegie mozzarella with basil & cherry tomatoes

Makes 12 hors d'oeuvres

Ciliegie means "cherries" in Italian—because the mozzarella is formed into cherry-size balls. I like that it also refers to the cherry tomatoes in the recipe. This bite-sized hors d'oeuvre is inspired by a wonderful summer salad the Italians call *insalata caprese* (a salad of fresh mozzarella, tomatoes, and basil).

6 cherry tomatoes, cut into halves

12 fresh basil leaves, cut into halves

6 ciliegie mozzarella balls, cut into halves

Salt and pepper

¼ cup balsamic vinegar

¼ cup extra-virgin olive oil

1 teaspoon minced garlic (optional)

Spear one half of one cherry tomato on a toothpick. Next, spear two halves of a fresh basil leaf, followed by one half of a mozzarella ball. Repeat for all 12 hors d'oeuvres, and season with salt and pepper. Arrange on a tray and serve with the balsamic vinegar and olive oil (I like to offer them separately) on the side for dipping. Add the minced garlic to the olive oil for an extra layer of flavor.

shrimp & crab bisque with parmesan croutons

Makes 10–12 hors d'oeuvre–size servings

I serve this creamy soup in lots of different ways. In the Holiday Toast, I used it as an hors d'oeuvre, presenting it in elegant small glasses, but this recipe can serve up to six people as an appetizer course before a meal, or four for a main course (try serving it over white rice).

2 pounds jumbo shrimp, heads on

6 tablespoons butter

1 cup roughly chopped yellow onion

1 medium carrot, peeled and chopped roughly

1 red bell pepper, seeds and ribs removed,
    chopped roughly

2 cloves garlic, chopped roughly

4 cups chicken stock

1 cup canned crushed tomatoes

2 sprigs tarragon

1 bay leaf

1 teaspoon cayenne pepper

¼ cup fino sherry

¼ cup Grand Marnier

2 tablespoons flour

1 pound lump crabmeat

16 ounces light or fat-free evaporated milk

Salt and pepper

1 recipe Parmesan Croutons (right)

Fresh cilantro leaves, for garnish

Peel, devein, and rinse the shrimp, then pat them dry, chop them into small pieces, and set aside. Reserve the shells.

In a large stockpot, melt the butter over medium heat. Add the onion and sauté until it is tender and translucent, about 3 minutes. Add the carrot, bell pepper, garlic, and shrimp shells and sauté for another 8 minutes, until all the vegetables are soft.

Add the chicken stock, tomatoes, tarragon, bay leaf, and cayenne pepper. Carefully add the sherry and Grand Marnier, and stir. Bring the mixture to a boil, then reduce the heat to a simmer and cook for 40 minutes. Strain the mixture into a clean pot and place it over medium heat.

Add the flour slowly, using a whisk to stir, and simmer for another 5 minutes. Add the shrimp and crabmeat and cook for another 5 minutes. Take the pan off the heat and add the evaporated milk, stirring to incorporate. Season to taste with salt and pepper. Garnish with Parmesan Croutons and top with a sprinkle of cilantro.

PARMESAN CROUTONS

Can be made a day ahead, and kept covered in an airtight container.

6 slices good white bread, crusts removed,
    and cut into ½-inch cubes

2 tablespoons olive oil

1 teaspoon garlic powder

Salt

¼ cup grated Parmesan cheese

Preheat oven to 400°F.

Toss the bread cubes with the olive oil. Combine the garlic powder, salt, and Parmesan, and sprinkle over the bread, gently tossing to coat. Arrange the cubes in a single layer on a baking sheet, and bake till golden brown, turning them as necessary (8 to 10 minutes).

go-to guacamole

Serves 6

This is an instant homemade appetizer for any time. Serve it with a big bowl of good tortilla chips and Homemade Fresh Salsa (right) or your favorite store-bought brand.

3 ripe Hass avocados

Juice of ½ lemon

Juice of 2 limes (¼ cup)

2 tablespoons chopped green chilis (optional— use them if you like it spicy!)

Salt and pepper

Peel and mash the avocados in a large mixing bowl. Squeeze the lemon juice over the avocado to keep it from browning. Stir in the lime juice and chilis, if you like (or serve the chilis on the side), and season with salt and pepper to finish.

homemade fresh salsa

Serves 4–6

The key to success with this deliciously simple salsa is to use the best tomatoes you can get. Their sweet flavor, combined with the crunchy onions and bright cilantro, makes a perfect match for crisp tortilla chips or as an accent to any Southwestern dish. Try it with Arroz con Pollo, page 143.

2 cups chopped tomatoes

1 small white onion, finely diced

3 tablespoons chopped cilantro

Salt

Mix all the ingredients together and serve with chips and guacamole or with the Quick Quesadillas (page 131).

tip

CHOOSING AND WORKING WITH AVOCADOS

A ripe avocado should feel slightly soft (but not mushy). Its peel should appear more charcoal than green. (Hass avocados—the best choice—have a pebbly surface, rather than smooth skin.) To prepare your avocados, make a cut lengthwise all around the fruit. Pull the halves apart and use a spoon to remove the pit. For guacamole, simply scoop the flesh out of its skin. Peel the avocado if you want to slice or dice it. Before mashing or slicing avocado, squeeze lemon juice on it to help keep it from browning.

quick quesadillas

Serves 8

These quesadillas make a nice lunch or snack served with a salad. You can add ground beef or shredded chicken as well, if you like, along with a few slices of pickled jalapeños if you're feeling spicy.

½ cup canned refried beans

8 medium flour tortillas

¼ pound Monterey Jack cheese, grated

¼ pound Cheddar cheese, grated

2 tablespoons olive oil

Fresh salsa, for serving

Sour cream, for serving

Spread refried beans on each of the tortillas. On 4 tortillas, sprinkle enough of each cheese to cover the tortilla, leaving a little space at the edge. Cover with the remaining 4 tortillas, bean-side pressed against the cheese. In a medium skillet on medium-high heat, warm the olive oil, then cook the tortillas one at a time until they're golden brown on both sides and the cheese is melted. Slice into quarters and serve with fresh salsa on top and sour cream on the side.

emmentaler & gruyère fondue

Serves 6

1 clove garlic, smashed, peeled, and cut in half

1½ cups crisp white wine

½ pound Gruyère, grated roughly

½ pound Emmentaler, grated roughly

1 tablespoon cornstarch

1 tablespoon kirsch, a cherry brandy (optional)

1 teaspoon ground nutmeg

Grapes, pears, apples, and other fruits, cut into cubes, if needed

Cooked baby potatoes, vegetables such as broccoli, cauliflower, and bell peppers, cut into bite-size pieces

1 baguette, or other crusty artisan loaf, cut into bite-size cubes

Rub the inside of a thick sauce pot with the garlic clove to coat the pan with garlic flavor. Pour in the white wine and bring to a simmer over medium heat.

While the wine is heating up, in a large mixing bowl, toss the grated Gruyère and Emmentaler with the cornstarch, so that the cornstarch coats the cheese (this will help with the texture of the fondue).

Add the cheese to the wine gradually, stirring to incorporate until the cheese is creamy. Pour in the kirsch. Add the nutmeg and stir. Transfer the fondue to your fondue pot and keep it warm over a small flame. Serve with long skewers and the fruits, vegetables, and breads for dipping.

hot wings with pineapple glaze & creamy blue cheese dip

Makes 16 pieces

These are a staple for parties at my house. I like drumettes because they are so meaty, but you could substitute wings, with the tips removed, if you prefer. You can make the pineapple glaze and the blue cheese dip ahead of time and keep them in the fridge for a day or two. If you want your wings less spicy, omit the hot sauce from the glaze.

1½ cups pineapple juice

¼ cup hot sauce

1 tablespoon chili paste

1 tablespoon light corn syrup

16 chicken drumettes (small drumsticks)

Salt and pepper

2 tablespoons hot chili powder

1 tablespoon garlic powder

1 tablespoon Chinese five-spice powder

1 tablespoon crushed red pepper flakes

1 cup flour

2 tablespoons vegetable oil

6 stalks celery, trimmed and cut into 4-inch sticks

1 cup baby carrots

1 recipe Creamy Blue Cheese Dip (see 133)

In a saucepan over medium heat, combine the pineapple juice, hot sauce, and chili paste. Bring to a boil, then lower heat to a simmer. Add the corn syrup and simmer until the mixture is reduced by half (approximately 15 minutes). Let the pineapple glaze cool, then refrigerate it for at least an hour or up to two days.

Preheat the oven to 425°F.

Rinse the chicken, pat dry, and arrange pieces on a platter. Season with salt and pepper. In a small bowl, combine the chili powder, garlic powder, and Chinese five-spice. Rub the spice mixture onto the drumettes, turning to coat lightly (more spice will make them more spicy). Sprinkle the red pepper flakes over all the chicken pieces.

Spread the flour onto a plate or shallow bowl and dredge the spice-coated drumettes in flour to coat, shaking off any excess.

In a large skillet, heat the vegetable oil. Add the chicken pieces and brown them for 3 minutes on each side (you may need to brown the chicken in batches if your pan isn't big enough). When the chicken is crispy, transfer the pieces to a baking pan.

Brush the chicken pieces with the pineapple glaze and bake them for approximately 20 minutes, glazing and turning them every 5 minutes. Place the pan under the broiler for 3 to 5 minutes, or until the chicken skin is crispy and the glaze is caramelized slightly.

Serve warm or at room temperature with celery sticks, baby carrots, Creamy Blue Cheese Dip, and, of course, lots of napkins!

CREAMY BLUE CHEESE DIP

Serves 6–8

If you're in a pinch, you can always add some fresh crumbled blue cheese to a high-quality bottled blue cheese dip, but this recipe is really worth the extra few minutes.

1 cup sour cream

1 cup crumbled blue cheese (I like Gorgonzola or Roquefort)

5 tablespoons mayonnaise

1 teaspoon garlic powder

Salt and pepper

In a large bowl, combine all the ingredients except the salt and pepper. Don't overstir—you want to keep the chunkiness of the crumbled blue cheese. Season to taste with salt and pepper. Keep refrigerated until ready to serve.

baby arugula salad with grapefruit & avocado

Serves 6 as a side salad

I love the creaminess of avocado combined with the bright flavors of grapefruit and tender baby arugula. This salad would also work well with baby spinach.

6-ounce package baby arugula

½ cup fresh or canned grapefruit sections, cut into small pieces

1 Hass avocado

1 lemon, halved

¼ cup extra-virgin olive oil

Salt and pepper

Rinse and dry the arugula and place it in a large bowl. Add the grapefruit pieces. Peel, pit, and cut the avocado into 1-inch chunks. Squeeze a little lemon juice on it to keep it from browning. Drizzle the olive oil and squeeze more lemon juice over the salad. Add salt and pepper and toss.

asian noodle salad with peanut dressing

Serves 6

You will love the sweet and spicy balance of flavors in this dish. Of course, you can eliminate the chili paste if you like it milder.

12 ounces Chinese-style wheat noodles

2 tablespoons sesame oil, plus more for the just-cooked noodles

½ cup peanut butter (smooth or crunchy)

Juice of 2 limes (¼ cup)

1 tablespoon Asian-style chili paste

2 tablespoons sugar

1 cup firm tofu, cut into small cubes

1 cup bean sprouts

1 cup finely shredded carrots

Fresh cilantro leaves, for garnish

In a large pot of salted boiling water, cook noodles according to package instructions. Drain and rinse in cold water. Toss noodles in a few dashes of sesame oil to prevent sticking, and reserve.

Place peanut butter, lime juice, sesame oil, chili paste, and sugar in a small bowl and mix well.

Combine tofu, bean sprouts, carrots, and noodles in a large bowl, and pour peanut sauce over all. Toss well to coat.

Garnish with fresh cilantro. May be served chilled or at room temperature.

sweet & spicy parmesan popcorn

Serves 6 as a snack—or just me

The marriage of salty Parmesan and sweet brown sugar is a match made in heaven, if you ask me. One fateful day I discovered this combo, and I've never looked back. I've even smuggled it into the movies.

1 package plain microwave popcorn

4 tablespoons (½ stick) butter

3 tablespoons brown sugar

½ cup good-quality grated Parmesan cheese

1 teaspoon crushed red pepper flakes

Prepare the popcorn according to package instructions. Melt the butter in a small saucepan. Combine the brown sugar, Parmesan, and red pepper flakes in a small bowl.

To keep butter from making the popcorn soggy, transfer the melted butter into a small spray bottle, misting the popcorn while tossing it in the bowl. (I promise it's worth it, but if you don't do this, add the butter slowly, a teaspoon at a time, while tossing.) Sprinkle the Parmesan mixture over the popcorn, tossing to coat.

LAST-MINUTE HORS D'OEUVRES INSPIRATIONS

I am the queen of last-minute hors d'oeuvres. Usually I plan to make a bunch of things, and then I run out of time and have to come up with something impressive on the fly. But I've discovered some of my favorite hors d'oeuvres by combining high-quality, store-bought ingredients in delicious, eye-appealing ways. The key is in the quality of the elements used, so aim for the best whenever possible. Instant nibbles, here we come!

jalapeño shrimp cocktail

Buy a quarter pound of cooked, peeled medium shrimp for each guest you expect. For a party of 8 guests, pour one 6 to 8-ounce bottle of your favorite seafood cocktail sauce into a shallow bowl. Mix 1 tablespoon of pickled sliced jalapeños and 2 tablespoons sour cream into the cocktail sauce and serve with the shrimp and fresh lemon wedges.

parmesan breadsticks

Preheat the oven to 400°F. On a parchment-lined baking sheet, arrange a single layer of store-bought plain breadsticks. Drizzle them with olive oil and sprinkle them with freshly grated Parmesan cheese. Add a dash of freshly ground black pepper and bake the breadsticks for about 5 minutes, or until the cheese is melted and golden brown. Let the sticks cool and serve them with a simple, slightly chilled red wine or rosé.

tequila-soaked olives with blue cheese

Buy a jar of good olives and a hunk of blue cheese (I like Spanish Cabrales or French Roquefort). Toss the olives in a bowl with a splash of tequila and a squeeze of lime. Cut the cheese into small chunks and spear toothpicks with one olive and one blue cheese chunk each. Make up a batch of Margaritas Más Grandes (page 191) and say "olé!"

mozzarella bocconcini with hot pepper oil & basil

Look for tiny fresh bocconcini or ciliegie (miniature balls) of mozzarella at your gourmet store. Drain them, place them in a shallow bowl, drizzle with hot chili oil, and sprinkle with fresh chopped basil. Provide toothpicks for picking up the cheese.

goat cheese with walnuts & honey

Buy a large slice of good goat cheese. Unwrap it and press one flat side of the cheese into a plate of finely crushed walnuts. Place the cheese on a pretty plate walnut side up and finish with a spoonful of clover honey and a crack of fresh black pepper.

mini salami focaccia melts

Preheat your oven to 400°F. Slice a store-bought focaccia loaf in half lengthwise. On the bottom half, drizzle extra-virgin olive oil. Arrange thin slices of salami (I like the slightly spicy soppressata), and top the salami with shredded mozzarella cheese. Drizzle balsamic vinegar on the top half of the loaf and place over the bottom half. Bake the loaf on a foil-lined baking sheet until the cheese melts, 8 to 10 minutes. Slice the focaccia into 2-inch squares and serve with Italian beer and good pickles.

For the bigger events my company creates, we've set up kitchens in places you can't imagine—closets, hallways, even a barn! Chefs are used to preparing large quantities of good food with limited resources. • But parties at home are different. One of my colleagues told me about a private catering job she did for a small dinner party in a client's home. The menu included fish baked in parchment paper. When the guest count

main courses

suddenly increased, she found herself "in the weeds" as we say in the business. Why? Because a home oven can't accommodate a dozen parchment packages, and if you cook them separately, the quality of the dish will be inconsistent. When it comes to party foods, especially main courses, you want things that can be prepared for a larger group without renting a convection oven! All the dishes in this section are group-friendly, with elements you can prepare a bit in advance.

oven-roasted halibut
with cherry tomatoes & thyme

Serves 6

Halibut is a meaty yet light fish, and the brightness of the tomatoes pairs beautifully with the fresh oregano. The herb butter helps the flavor of the thyme really shine through.

6 tablespoons butter at room temperature, plus 2 tablespoons for sautéing

12 sprigs thyme, plus 1 tablespoon chopped

1 large savoy cabbage (about 2 pounds), finely shredded

1 bunch scallions, thinly sliced

6 halibut fillets, about 5 ounces each

Salt and pepper

Juice of 2 lemons (¼ cup)

½ cup Sauvignon Blanc, or other dry white wine

½ pint cherry tomatoes, sliced in half

In a small bowl, combine the butter and the chopped thyme, mixing to incorporate the herbs. If you like, spoon the herb butter into the center of a piece of parchment or wax paper and roll it into a log shape. Chill the butter for at least an hour for easy slicing. If you don't want to make the butter log, just chill the butter in a bowl covered with plastic (it won't look as good, but the butter is going to melt in the oven anyway).

Preheat the oven to 425°F. Melt the remaining 2 tablespoons of the butter in a large pan, and sauté the cabbage and scallions over medium heat until tender, about 6 minutes. Portion the cooked cabbage into 6 equal piles in a casserole dish.

Place a fillet on each pile of cabbage, season with salt and pepper, and drizzle with lemon juice and white wine. Cut the prepared herb butter into 6 equal-sized pats, and place one on top of each fillet. Scatter halved tomatoes evenly around the fillets. Top each piece of fish with 2 sprigs of thyme. Cover the casserole with foil and bake for 20 minutes.

coconut chicken curry

Serves 6

This curry is so wonderfully fragrant, you might have trouble waiting for your guests to arrive before sampling it yourself. Recently, I was carrying a batch of it over to a potluck party at a friend's house and five total strangers stopped me along the way to ask what smelled so good. It's the spices and the sweetness of the coconut milk. Have I mentioned I am in love with coconut milk? It's one of my favorite ingredients (I use it to cook rice and couscous as well).

2½ pounds chicken thighs and drumsticks

½ cup flour

3 tablespoons vegetable oil

1 onion, chopped

3 cloves garlic, minced

12-ounce can unsweetened coconut milk

3 cups chicken stock

Juice of 2 limes (¼ cup)

½ teaspoon ground cardamom

1 teaspoon cayenne pepper

1 teaspoon curry powder

3 tablespoons Asian-style chili paste

¼ cup diced tomatoes

Salt

Dredge the chicken pieces in flour. Heat the oil in a large pot or Dutch oven and cook the chicken until the skin is golden, about 4 minutes on each side. Set aside chicken and reserve.

Add the onion and garlic to the pot and gently cook them until the onion is tender and translucent. Return chicken to the pot and cover with coconut milk and chicken stock. Stir in the lime juice. Add the cardamom, cayenne, curry powder, chili paste, and tomatoes, and simmer gently for 30 to 45 minutes. Add salt to taste. Serve with rice or Parsley Couscous (see page 167).

arroz con pollo

Serves 6–8

This recipe is a shortcut to a one-pot meal. I use organic rotisserie chicken from my local market, but of course you can roast your own, if you prefer.

2 tablespoons butter

1 medium Spanish onion, chopped

2 tablespoons minced garlic

2 cups long-grain white rice

3 cups chicken stock

1 cup white wine

2 tablespoons adobo seasoning

½ teaspoon saffron

¼ cup chopped roasted red peppers

2 whole roasted chickens, cut up into pieces

½ cup green peas

¼ cup chopped green olives

16-ounce can black or pinto beans, drained, rinsed, and warmed for serving

In a large stockpot, Dutch oven, or deep skillet, melt the butter over medium heat and sauté the onion and garlic. Add the rice and stir. Add the stock, wine, adobo, saffron, and peppers and stir. Bring to a boil. Lower the heat and arrange the chicken pieces atop the rice. Simmer for 15 to 20 minutes, or until the rice is cooked. Add the peas and the olives, then stir and let the pot stand off the heat for another 5 or 10 minutes before serving with the beans on the side.

roasted maple-glazed cornish game hens

Serves 6

Roasting these Cornish hens is much easier (and quicker) than cooking a large turkey, and everyone gets drumsticks and breasts!

6 Cornish game hens

Salt and pepper

6 tablespoons butter

½ cup maple syrup

Preheat your oven to 425°F. Rinse the birds and pat dry. Season with salt and pepper and arrange in a roasting pan with deep sides.

In a saucepan, melt the butter and remove it from the heat. Pour the melted butter over the birds and put them in the oven, uncovered. Let them brown for 10 minutes.

In a mixing bowl, combine the maple syrup with ½ cup hot water. After the first 10 minutes, reduce the oven temperature to 325°F and baste the birds with one-third of the glaze, using a baster. Check the birds every 10 minutes, basting them each time. If they start to brown too much, cover the pan with foil and continue cooking for approximately 1 hour and 5 minutes (including the browning time), or until a meat thermometer reads 165°F when inserted into the meaty part of the thigh.

focaccia panini with prosciutto à la caprese

Serves 4

I am obsessed with my panini maker. I believe everyone should own one. Many of the new versions have two-sided cooking surfaces that allow you to use them as a griddle when you're not grilling pressed sandwiches. This panini is unique because it features focaccia, a dense, "quilty" Italian bread whose spongy texture soaks up flavor. I also like the fact that focaccia doesn't have an overly chewy crust—it's perfect for your picnic enjoyment!

1 store-bought focaccia (approximately 10 inches square and 2 inches thick)

3 tablespoons extra-virgin olive oil

2 tablespoons balsamic vinegar, plus additional for drizzling

¾ pound fresh mozzarella (use the best quality you can get)

3 vine-ripened tomatoes, sliced

4 ounces good-quality prosciutto

½ cup fresh arugula leaves

Salt and pepper

Slice the focaccia in half lengthwise, then cut each half into quarters, forming four tops and bottoms. (If you prefer smaller sandwiches, cut accordingly.) Using a pastry brush, coat the inside of the top and bottom layers with the olive oil. Brush the balsamic vinegar on each slice in the same way.

Arrange the bottom slices on a tray and layer the ingredients on them one at a time. Start with the mozzarella, then top with the tomato, the prosciutto, and the arugula. Season with salt and pepper to taste and drizzle with a little more vinegar, if you like. Add the top slices to close the sandwiches, and grill on your panini press until the mozzarella is melted, about 2 minutes. If you don't have a panini press, place the paninis on a grill pan or griddle and press them with the bottom of a heavy skillet covered in aluminum foil. Serve warm or at room temperature.

world's best chili

Serves 10 (and freezes well, if you have leftovers)

I have some sports fans in my life, and the first time I made this chili it was for a Super Bowl party. It was such a hit, folks now request it! This dish can be made in advance and kept in the fridge for a couple of days or frozen for a month or so. I like to make a big batch, then freeze it in small containers to take for lunch or to serve with rice for dinner.

3 pounds ground beef

Salt and pepper

2 tablespoons vegetable oil

1 medium yellow onion, chopped

24-ounce can tomato puree

3 cups beef stock

¼ cup red wine vinegar

2 tablespoons pickled sliced jalapeño peppers
    (optional)

1 tablespoon ground nutmeg

1 tablespoon plus 1 teaspoon ground cumin

1 tablespoon garlic powder

1 tablespoon cayenne pepper

10¾-ounce can pinto beans, drained

10¾-ounce can kidney beans, drained

2 cups shredded Monterey Jack or cheddar
    cheese, for serving

2 cups sour cream, for serving

Season the beef with the salt and pepper. Heat the oil in a large saucepan and brown the beef. Remove beef and set aside. Discard all but 2 tablespoons of fat from the pan. Add the onion and sauté until translucent and fragrant.

Return the beef to the pan and add the tomato puree, beef stock, vinegar, jalapeños (if using), and spices and simmer for 30 minutes. Adjust the seasoning, adding more salt and pepper, if needed. Add the beans and cook for an additional 15 minutes.

Serve in mugs or bowls with cheese and sour cream on top.

brother david's grilled chicken & ribs

Serves 10

Brother David is my brother David, the one whose backyard I am always borrowing. He loves to grill and we all love it when he does! Hey, the sauce is my recipe, though, so don't give him credit for that.

¼ cup olive oil

3 pounds chicken pieces, skin on (thighs, drumsticks, breasts)

3 pounds pork ribs on the slab

Salt and pepper to taste

¼ cup garlic powder

2 recipes Sweet & Tangy Barbecue Sauce (see right)

Lightly brush your grill with olive oil and preheat it to approximately 350°F.

In the meantime, rinse the meat, pat it dry, and season with salt, pepper, and garlic powder. Arrange the chicken and ribs on the grill. Resist turning the meat for at least 5 minutes. This will help it sear nicely. After 5 minutes or so, turn the meat over, sear the other side for 5 more minutes. Turn again, and this time, brush the meat with the barbecue sauce. Then turn again every 5 minutes, repeating the process of brushing the meat with sauce until the chicken and ribs are cooked through and the barbecue sauce begins to caramelize and form a crust on the meat (35 to 40 minutes).

Serve with more barbecue sauce on the side.

SWEET & TANGY BARBECUE SAUCE

This recipe yields enough sauce to glaze three pounds of meat. We doubled it for the chicken and ribs at our barbecue party. You'll use about half to marinate and glaze the meat while cooking, and the rest as a condiment on the buffet for those who like it really saucy.

1 tablespoon vegetable oil

1 large yellow onion, minced

2 cups ketchup

8-ounce jar honey mustard

2 tablespoons minced garlic

¼ cup brown sugar

½ cup cider vinegar

2 tablespoons Worcestershire sauce

Heat the oil in a large saucepan and cook the onion until tender and translucent. Add all remaining ingredients and simmer for 10 minutes. Remove the sauce from the heat and use a handheld blender to process it to a smooth paste. (Alternatively, transfer it to an upright blender.) Return to pan and simmer gently for an additional 5 minutes.

Separate the sauce into two containers. Use one to marinate and glaze the meat during grilling. Reserve the remainder for use as a sauce at the table.

pineapple-glazed shrimp kebabs

Serves 10

This is the ultimate summery seafood dish. It would be great with the Parsley Couscous or the Baby Arugula Salad with Grapefruit & Avocado.

Vegetable oil, for the grill

4 bell peppers, assorted colors, cut into 1½-inch squares

5 pounds jumbo shrimp, peeled and deveined

1 pound fresh pineapple chunks

1 recipe Pineapple Glaze (page 132)

3 limes, cut in wedges

Salt and pepper

Brush your grill with oil and preheat it to 325°F.

Soak about 20 bamboo skewers in cold water (this will keep them from burning on the grill).

To assemble the kebabs: spear a piece of bell pepper onto a skewer, followed by a shrimp, a pineapple chunk, and another piece of pepper. Each skewer should hold 3 shrimp and several contrasting colors of bell pepper. Repeat until all ingredients are used. Season with salt and pepper.

Place the assembled kebabs on the hot grill and brush them with pineapple glaze. Cook for 3 minutes on each side, turning and glazing them once. Serve with lime wedges.

red miso–baked salmon with scallions

Serves 6

This is one of my go-to dishes for when I have company. The miso-and-soy blend is a salty and slightly sweet foil for the meatiness of the salmon.

¼ cup red miso paste

¼ cup soy sauce (use the low-sodium version, if you like)

2 tablespoons rice wine vinegar

1 tablespoon sesame oil

6 salmon fillets, about 6 ounces each

2 scallions, sliced thinly

Preheat the oven to 400°F.

In a small bowl, combine the miso with the soy sauce, mixing in the liquid slowly. Add the rice wine vinegar, stirring well. Finally, stir in the sesame oil slowly.

Arrange the salmon fillets on a foil-lined baking dish. Brush each fillet with the red miso glaze, then pour the rest of the glaze over the fish. Top each piece of fish with a few slices of scallion, and bake, covered with foil, for 15 minutes.

Uncover and bake for another 10 minutes, or until the salmon is cooked to your desired doneness and the scallions become caramelized. Plate each fillet and drizzle sauce from the dish over the top.

white lasagna with wild mushrooms

Serves 6

You can substitute light versions of all the dairy ingredients here if you like (although I prefer freshly made full-fat ricotta), but definitely look for really great mushrooms at your farmers' market or grocery.

2 tablespoons olive oil, plus additional for the baking dish

1 medium yellow onion, minced

1¼ pounds wild mushrooms, washed, woody stems removed, and chopped

½ cup white wine

1 egg

1 pound ricotta cheese

¾ pound dry lasagna noodles

2 cups shredded Gouda cheese

½ cup grated Parmesan cheese

Salt and pepper

Preheat the oven to 375°F. In a sauté pan, heat the olive oil. Add the onion and cook till it is translucent. Add the mushrooms and sauté till they soften, about 3 minutes. Add the white wine and reduce, about 5 minutes, then remove mushrooms from the heat.

In a bowl, beat the egg lightly. Add the ricotta and mix. Set aside.

Prepare your lasagna noodles according to package instructions.

Grease an 8-by-12-inch baking pan with olive oil. Place a small amount of the mushroom mixture on the bottom of the pan. Add a layer of pasta, overlapping slightly. Top the noodles with one quarter of the mushrooms, followed by one quarter of the ricotta, one quarter of the Gouda, and one quarter of the Parmesan cheese. Season with salt and pepper. Add a layer of pasta. Repeat the process, using one half of each of the remaining ingredients. For your final (third) layer, use the rest of the ingredients.

Bake the lasagna, covered with foil, for 55 minutes. Remove the foil and bake for another 5 to 10 minutes, or until the cheese is melted and golden brown. Let stand for at least 10 to 15 minutes before serving.

seared fillet of beef with foie gras chapeau & balsamic pan sauce

Serves 6

This dish is luxurious. If you're not into foie gras, the beef is wonderful by itself or served with Truffled Mashed Potatoes and Creamed Spinach Royale.

4 tablespoons (½ stick) butter

6 fillets of beef, about 4 ounces each

Salt and pepper

½ cup balsamic vinegar

7-ounce block (canned) foie gras, cut into 6 equal-sized medallions

2 tablespoons chives, chopped finely

Melt 2 tablespoons of the butter in a skillet large enough to hold all of the fillets. Season the beef with salt and pepper and sear in the butter until a rich brown—3 minutes on each side for rare, 5 minutes on each side for medium-rare. Set aside.

Deglaze the pan with balsamic vinegar, stirring well with a wooden spoon to incorporate all the beef flavor. Allow to reduce for about 2 minutes and then whisk in the remaining 2 tablespoons butter. Remove from heat and cover with foil to keep warm.

Heat a nonstick skillet until it is very hot. Carefully place 2 medallions of foie gras in the pan. After 1 minute, flip each medallion with a spatula (the edges and surface should be well-seared). Remove the foie gras after an additional minute and repeat with the remaining pieces.

To serve, top each fillet with a piece of foie gras. Drizzle with a small amount of the balsamic pan sauce, and finish with a sprinkle of chives.

Side dishes make the meal for me. I would rather have less of the main stuff and more of the accompaniments. Some of the dishes in this section would make a whole delicious meal by themselves or in combination with each other. • When you're planning side dishes for a party or a meal, think about how to

on the side

balance the flavors, colors, and types of ingredients. (You wouldn't want to serve rice and pasta on the same plate, or three dishes that feature cheddar cheese, for example.) For a tasty balance on your party plate, pair sides that are earthy or creamy with those that are crisp or tangy.

haricots verts with lemon & parmesan

Serves 6–8

These elegant green beans make a perfect accompaniment to a picnic lunch or dinner.

1 pound haricots verts, rinsed, with stem ends
    snapped off
Juice of 2 lemons (¼ cup)
2 tablespoons olive oil
¼ cup Parmesan cheese
Salt and pepper

In a wide skillet, bring 3 cups water to a rolling boil. Drop the beans into the water and remove the pan from the heat. Let the beans sit in the hot water for up to 2 minutes, then drain and rinse them under very cold water (or dunk them in a bath of ice water). Toss the beans with the other ingredients and keep refrigerated until ready to go.

radicchio & carrot slaw

Serves 8

This wonderful slaw is a great twist on classic cole-slaw. If you like your slaw crunchier, make it just before the party.

2 heads radicchio, cut in half, then sliced thinly
⅔ cup mayonnaise
2 tablespoons sugar
1 teaspoon dried fennel seed
¾ cup roughly grated or julienned carrots
⅓ cup white wine vinegar
Salt and pepper

In a large mixing bowl, toss all the ingredients together. Serve chilled.

stewed okra, peas & tomatoes

Serves 6 as a side dish

This stewed vegetarian dish makes a wonderful accompaniment to any meal, but it can also be a meal in itself, served with couscous and salad. You can keep this dish in the fridge for a day or two.

2 tablespoons butter

½ cup chopped yellow onion

8 ounces tomato paste

¾ cup chopped fresh okra

1½ cups chopped fresh tomatoes

2 cups fresh organic peas (or frozen peas)

¼ cup finely chopped green chilis

1 teaspoon garlic powder

½ teaspoon ground coriander

Salt and pepper

In a sauté pan, heat the butter over medium heat. Add the onion and cook until translucent. Add the tomato paste and stir. Add the okra, tomatoes, peas, chilis, garlic powder, and coriander. Stir, season with salt and pepper, and simmer for 10 minutes, stirring occasionally. The vegetables should be soft but not mushy.

grilled southwestern corn on the cob

Serves 8

This is simply the best corn ever—I love how charred it gets on the grill. But if you don't have a grill, you can boil the corn in water for 3 minutes, then add the toppings. If you like it spicy, add a pinch of cayenne at the end.

2 tablespoons olive oil, plus additional for the grill

8 ears fresh corn on the cob, shucked and cleaned

½ cup mayonnaise

Salt

½ cup grated Parmesan cheese

Fresh cilantro leaves, for garnish

Preheat your grill and brush it with oil. Brush each ear of corn with oil and grill for approximately 5 minutes, turning occasionally, until the ears are slightly charred.

Remove the corn from the grill and spread mayo on each ear. Season lightly with salt, then sprinkle with the Parmesan cheese, turning the ears to coat. Garnish with fresh cilantro leaves.

creamed spinach royale

Serves 6–8

You can make this delicious spinach recipe up to two days in advance, and reheat it in a skillet or casserole dish.

8 tablespoons (1 stick) butter

1 large yellow onion, chopped

2 tablespoons flour

1 teaspoon ground nutmeg

1 cup heavy cream

¾ cup grated Parmesan cheese, plus more if needed

1 pound frozen spinach, thawed and drained

Salt and pepper

Melt the butter. Add the onion and sauté until it is translucent (3 to 5 minutes). Add the flour and nutmeg and stir to form a smooth paste. Cook for approximately 1 minute, then add the cream and Parmesan cheese, cooking for another 2 to 3 minutes, until you have a thick, creamy sauce.

Add the spinach to the pan and season with salt and pepper. Cook until the spinach is warmed through, then season to taste with more cheese or salt as you desire.

truffled mashed potatoes

Serves 6–8

It's amazing how a little drizzle of truffle oil will transform simple mashed potatoes into an earthy, elegant accompaniment. My other secret ingredient is the sour cream.

2 pounds russet potatoes, peeled and quartered

¼ cup sour cream

4 tablespoons (½ stick) butter

Salt and pepper

2 tablespoons truffle oil

Chopped fresh parsley, for garnish

Place the potatoes in a pot of salted water and boil until cooked through, about 15 minutes. Drain them and mash in an electric mixer or by hand. Add the sour cream and butter and mix well, seasoning to taste with salt and pepper. When the potatoes are well mixed (I like mine just a little lumpy), add the truffle oil and stir. Garnish with fresh parsley just before serving.

Note: Transform this dish into something even more special by sautéing 1 cup finely chopped mushrooms, such as shiitake or crimini, in 2 tablespoons of olive oil or butter. Season the mushrooms with salt and pepper and add them to the potatoes when you mash them.

potato, sausage & gruyère gratin

Serves 6–8

You could serve this potato gratin at almost any meal—with a breakfast or brunch, as a stand-alone lunch, or with a big salad for dinner. The tangy Gruyère is so delicious with the sausage and potatoes! You can make this dish a day or two ahead and just reheat it before serving.

3 breakfast sausage links (pork or turkey)

1 pound russet potatoes

1 pound Yukon Gold potatoes

Salt and pepper

3 tablespoons butter

1 medium yellow onion, chopped

¾ cup heavy cream (or substitute light)

2 teaspoons fresh tarragon leaves

½ pound Gruyère cheese, grated

Preheat the oven to 400°F. Heat a medium-sized nonstick skillet over medium-high heat. Squeeze the sausages from their casings into the skillet, breaking up the meat into small pieces. Brown the sausage meat, then remove the pan from the heat. Drain off the fat and reserve the meat.

Peel and grate the potatoes roughly using a box grater, being careful not to grate too finely, as this can make the potatoes too starchy. Combine the two types of potatoes in a large mixing bowl, season with salt and pepper, and reserve.

Add 2 tablespoons of the butter to the skillet used to cook the meat and sauté the onion until it is tender and translucent (3 to 5 minutes). Add the grated potatoes and sauté over medium-high heat until they are golden brown. Resist the temptation to stir the potatoes too much. Let them get really crisp.

Add the sausage back to the pan with the potatoes, then stir in the cream and the tarragon. Season with salt and pepper and cook for approximately 5 minutes over medium heat, until the cream reduces slightly. Add all but 2 tablespoons of the Gruyère and stir until the cheese is melted.

Butter a baking dish with the remaining tablespoon butter. Transfer the potato mixture to the dish. Sprinkle the remaining Gruyère on top and bake for about 10 minutes, or until the cheese is melted and golden brown. Serve warm.

baby romaine salad with corn, cucumber & cilantro vinaigrette

Serves 6

The bright flavors in this salad combined with the mellow baby romaine provide a nice foil to spicy dishes like World's Best Chili (page 146) or Hot Wings with Pineapple Glaze (page 132), but this refreshing salad would also make a great accompaniment to a grilled chicken breast or the baby lamb chops (page 123).

10 ounces packaged organic baby romaine greens, washed and dried

½ cup whole kernel corn, fresh or canned

1 cup peeled, chopped cucumber

Salt and pepper

1 recipe Cilantro Vinaigrette (see right)

Combine the romaine, corn, and cucumber and toss, adding salt and pepper to taste. Dress with the Cilantro Vinaigrette just before serving, or serve the dressing on the side.

CILANTRO VINAIGRETTE

¼ cup fresh cilantro leaves, washed and dried, with stems removed

1 clove garlic

2 tablespoons white wine vinegar

½ cup extra-virgin olive oil

Salt and pepper

In the bowl of a food processor, combine the cilantro, garlic, and vinegar and pulse a few times to mix. While pulsing, slowly add the olive oil through the top of the food processor until the mixture is emulsified. Add salt and pepper to taste.

For a little extra crunch, mix in Parmesan Croutons, page 127.

manchego jalapeño cornbread

Serves 8–12

Spicy, cheesy, and moist! I love this cornbread for dinner on a warm summer night, whether with barbecued meats or just a big old salad. If you don't have manchego, you can substitute cheddar, Monterey Jack, or Gouda.

1 cup cornmeal

1 cup all-purpose flour

6 ounces manchego cheese, grated

¼ cup granulated sugar

1 tablespoon baking powder

1 teaspoon salt

2 tablespoons pickled sliced jalapeño peppers

1 cup milk

⅓ cup vegetable oil

2 large eggs, lightly beaten

Preheat the oven to 400°F. Grease an 8-inch-square baking pan. Combine the cornmeal, flour, two-thirds of the manchego, the sugar, baking powder, and salt in a medium bowl. Mince 1 tablespoon of the jalapeños and combine with the milk, oil, and eggs in a small bowl; mix well. Add the milk mixture to the flour mixture and stir just until blended. Pour into the prepared pan.

Lay the remaining jalapeño slices on top of the batter approximately 3 inches apart (the idea is for each piece of cornbread to get a slice of jalapeño on top) and sprinkle with the remaining manchego. Bake for 20 to 25 minutes, or until a wooden pick inserted into center comes out clean. Serve warm.

classic herb stuffing

Serves 8

My mom used to make this stuffing with sliced white or whole wheat bread cut into cubes, but you could use a French bread or your favorite artisan loaf. If you want to make this dish vegetarian, substitute vegetable stock for the chicken stock.

8 tablespoons (1 stick) butter, melted
1 large onion, chopped finely
2 cups finely chopped celery
1 loaf day-old bread, chopped into ¾-inch cubes (10–12 cups)
½ cup raisins
1 teaspoon dried oregano
½ teaspoon ground sage
Salt and pepper
1½ cups chicken stock
¼ cup white wine vinegar

Preheat the oven to 350°F.

In a deep saucepan, add 2 tablespoons of the butter. Sweat the onion and celery until translucent. Add the bread cubes, raisins, herbs, and remaining butter, and stir to coat. Season with salt and pepper. Stir the liquids in gradually.

Transfer the stuffing to an oven dish and bake, covered, for 30 minutes. Remove cover and bake 5 to 10 minutes longer to create a crisper top.

cranberry clementine sauce

Serves 8

Clementines are smallish oranges that come into season in the colder months. Their juicy sweetness is a lovely foil to the tartness of cranberries.

Juice of 2 clementines (¼ cup)
½ cup sugar
1 pound fresh cranberries
Grated clementine zest, for garnish

In a saucepan, bring ½ cup water, the clementine juice, and the sugar to a boil, stirring to dissolve the sugar. Add the cranberries and return to a boil. Reduce the heat and simmer for 10 minutes, or until the cranberries burst.

Allow the sauce to come to room temperature and then chill it in the refrigerator. The sauce will thicken as it cools. Garnish with the clementine zest.

brussels sprouts with bacon & balsamic

Serves 8

I never liked Brussels sprouts as a kid, but now they are one of my favorites, especially paired with other comfort foods. This is a great side dish, or you could toss the whole thing in with a pound of pasta, sprinkle it with Parmesan cheese, and have a spectacular main course in no time!

2 tablespoons butter

¼ pound (4 strips) bacon, cut into ½-inch pieces

2 pounds Brussels sprouts, stalk ends removed, cut into halves, and blanched

¼ cup balsamic vinegar

Salt and pepper

In a large skillet, melt the butter over medium heat. Add the bacon and cook until crisp. Discard most of the fat, leaving 2 tablespoons in the pan.

Add the Brussels sprouts to the reserved fat in the pan, pour in the balsamic vinegar, and sauté until the vinegar caramelizes on the sprouts. Season with salt and pepper to taste.

baby potato salad with oregano

Serves 6

This is a perfect picnic salad. It would also be great with the Baby Lamb Chops (see page 123) or with the Oven-roasted Halibut (see page 140), for example.

2 pounds assorted baby potatoes (red, brown, and fingerling)

¼ cup extra-virgin olive oil

¼ cup white wine vinegar

3 tablespoons fresh oregano leaves

Salt and pepper

Place the potatoes in a pot of salted water. Bring to a boil and cook until tender. Drain the potatoes, rinse them under cold running water, and slice in half.

Transfer the potatoes to a large mixing bowl and pour the olive oil and white wine vinegar over them. Add oregano leaves and season with salt and pepper. Toss gently until the potatoes are evenly dressed.

cucumber raita with dill

Serves 8

I love to serve this on the side with spicy dishes such as Coconut Chicken Curry (page 142) or as a dip with crunchy fresh vegetables such as celery, carrots, broccoli, or cauliflower.

1 medium cucumber, peeled, seeded, and chopped
16-ounce tub yogurt, preferably Greek-style
2 tablespoons finely chopped fresh dill
Salt and pepper

In a mixing bowl, combine the cucumber and the yogurt. Stir in the dill. Season with salt and pepper to taste. Serve with crunchy vegetables such as broccoli, cauliflower, carrots, and celery, and with store-bought Indian naan (a doughy flat bread that is perfect for soaking up the creamy yogurt).

parsley couscous

Serves 6

Couscous is a wonderful side dish that is incredibly quick-cooking and light. This version is a perfect accompaniment to curries and fish dishes. Sometimes I substitute coconut milk for half the stock.

2 cups chicken or vegetable stock
1 teaspoon salt
1 cup couscous
1 tablespoon butter
¼ cup finely chopped fresh parsley

In a saucepan, bring the stock to a boil. Add the salt, couscous, and butter, stir, then remove the pan from the heat. Cover and wait 5 minutes. Uncover, fluff with a fork (do not stir), add the parsley, and serve. If you need to reheat or refluff the couscous, just add a teaspoon of olive oil and lightly mix with a fork.

cavatappi salad with peas, ricotta, basil & mint

Serves 8 as an appetizer or 4 as a main course

Cavatappi is a fabulous dried pasta. Its curly shape makes it ideal for sauces that cling to the pasta, like this ricotta paste with fresh mint. The ricotta sauce can also be used as a delicious dip.

1 pound dried cavatappi pasta

2 tablespoons extra-virgin olive oil

1 cup ricotta cheese

1 clove garlic, minced

1 cup fresh green peas (or frozen peas, thawed)

3 tablespoons chopped fresh mint

¼ cup chopped fresh basil

¼ cup pine nuts

Salt and pepper

2 tablespoons grated Parmesan cheese

In a large pot, bring salted water to a boil. Add the pasta and cook according to package directions. Two minutes before the pasta is finished cooking, add ½ cup of the peas to the pasta water. Drain the pasta and peas and set aside, mixing in 1 tablespoon of the olive oil to keep the pasta from sticking together.

Meanwhile, in a food processor, mix the ricotta, garlic, the remaining green peas, plus the mint and basil, until the mixture forms a paste. Add the remaining tablespoon of olive oil to the paste while it is processing.

When the pasta has cooled, toss in the ricotta paste and pine nuts and season with salt and pepper. Garnish with the Parmesan cheese. Serve at room temperature.

Breakfast is definitely my favorite meal. I love the combination of sweet and savory foods—French toast with syrup served alongside potatoes and bacon . . . divine! I've filled the following pages with some classics and a few twists to help jump start your day, whether you're hosting a party or just dining in bed! • When it comes to dessert, in my opinion, less is

breakfast & sweets

definitely not more. Quantities notwithstanding, I do tend to like my sweets on the simpler side, easy to prepare and more elemental in flavor. I prefer rustic dishes and seasonal, pure ingredients (with the occasional can of icing thrown in for balance!) so the following inspirations are mostly treats that can be made ahead and served simply, with style.

stuffed brioche french toast with mascarpone & chocolate

Serves 6

Brioche. Mascarpone. Melted chocolate. Need I say more? This is cloud nine stuff!

1 cup mascarpone cheese

½ cup sour cream

¼ cup granulated sugar

12 slices of brioche, 1½ inches thick, each cut into 2 triangles

12 ounces semisweet or dark chocolate chips

8 tablespoons (1 stick) butter

4 eggs, lightly beaten

¼ cup confectioners' sugar, for dusting

1 recipe Cherry Maple Syrup (see below)

In a medium-sized mixing bowl, combine the mascarpone, sour cream, and granulated sugar.

Cut into the long side of each triangle of brioche to create a pocket for the stuffing. Fill the pocket with the sweetened mascarpone mixture and about 2–3 tablespoons of chocolate chips.

Heat a large griddle or skillet over medium-high heat. Melt enough butter to coat the pan. While the butter is melting, soak the French toast in the beaten eggs, turning to coat the bread well. Sauté until golden brown, turning them as necessary.

Transfer the finished slices to a baking dish placed in a warm oven until you're ready to serve. Dust with confectioners' sugar and serve with the remaining butter and warm Cherry Maple Syrup.

CHERRY MAPLE SYRUP

1 cup good-quality maple syrup

¼ cup Cherry Syrup (see page 195), at room temperature

In a small saucepan over low heat, warm the maple syrup. Add the cherry syrup slowly, stirring to combine. Serve warm.

seasonal fruit salad with fresh mint

Serves 6

This can be a great dish year-round, if you choose the best fruits available. The addition of mint adds an unexpected, refreshing complement to the sweetness of the fruits.

1½ cups strawberries, cleaned and quartered

¾ cup fresh pineapple chunks

1 cup apples, cored and cut into chunks

1 pint blackberries, cleaned

¼ cup finely chopped mint

In a mixing bowl, combine the cut fruit and toss. Add the fresh mint and stir gently. Serve in parfait dishes or small bowls.

caramelized cinnamon banana bites

Serves 8 as a small dessert

These remind me of sweet plantains. I like to spoon them over vanilla ice cream while they are still warm, but they're great all by themselves. Be mindful that caramelized sugar gets very hot, so use caution while stirring and spooning the hot bananas.

6 tablespoons (¾ stick) butter

4 ripe bananas

1 teaspoon ground cinnamon

½ cup granulated sugar

¼ cup brown sugar

2 teaspoons confectioners' sugar

In the microwave, melt 4 tablespoons of the butter. Peel the bananas, slice them into small rounds, and toss them with the melted butter. In a large bowl, combine the cinnamon, granulated sugar, and brown sugar. Add the banana slices and coat them with the dry mixture. In a wide skillet, heat the remaining 2 tablespoons butter and add the bananas. Let them sauté until golden on one side, then turn them and cook until they are golden and caramelized on the other side.

When you're ready to serve dessert, sprinkle the bananas with the confectioners' sugar.

strawberry angel-food trifle

Serves 8

The good news: This delicious dessert can actually be very low fat if you use the low-fat or fat-free yogurt. The key is to use a good Greek yogurt—the flavor is amazingly rich, even in low-fat varieties. When you're assembling the dish, don't worry about creating perfect layers—this trifle is even prettier when the ingredients overlap a bit.

1 pound frozen strawberries

½ cup sugar

1 store-bought angel-food cake

16-ounce container fat-free or
    full-fat Greek yogurt

Place the strawberries and sugar in a saucepan. Heat gently until the strawberries are soft and the sugar has dissolved. Allow the juices to reduce by one quarter, or about 8 minutes. Let the strawberry mixture cool.

Tear fist-sized pieces from the angel-food cake and use them to line the bottom of a large, clear bowl or trifle dish. Cover with a layer of Greek yogurt and a layer of strawberries in syrup, filling in any holes in the previous layer. Add another layer of cake and continue building until all the ingredients have been used, ending with a few spoonfuls of yogurt and strawberries as a garnish.

pear apple crisp

Serves 6

3 apples, peeled, cored, and cut into
    1-inch cubes

3 pears, peeled, cored, and cut into
    1-inch cubes

¾ cup brown sugar

¼ cup granulated sugar

2 tablespoons lemon juice

¼ cup quick-cooking oats

¼ cup all-purpose flour

Pinch salt

Pinch cinnamon

4 tablespoons chilled butter, cut into
    small pieces

Preheat the oven to 375°F. Toss the fruit with ½ cup of the brown sugar, the granulated sugar, and lemon juice. Mix the remaining ¼ cup brown sugar and all other dry ingredients together. Add the butter, working it with your hands only until the ingredients begin to come together in a crumbly mixture.

Spoon the fruit mixture into 4-inch ramekins, filling them about three-quarters full. Place the ramekins on a baking tray to catch any overflow during cooking.

Sprinkle the topping over the fruit and bake the crisps for approximately 25 minutes. If the topping browns too quickly, cover the ramekins with foil.

Serve warm, with vanilla ice cream, if desired.

ice cream with amaretto & chocolate abstracts

Serves 6–8

The chocolate "abstracts" in this dish look very impressive, but they are easy things to make. After you melt the chocolate, let it cool a little before making the abstracts. A plastic funnel will help you pour the chocolate into the squeeze bottle without making a mess.

4 ounces semisweet or dark chocolate chips
2 pints vanilla or coffee ice cream
¼ cup amaretto

Line a baking sheet that will fit in your freezer with parchment or wax paper. Place the chocolate chips in a microwave-safe container and microwave on medium for 20 seconds. Stir and return to microwave for another 10 seconds. Chocolate burns easily, so check and stir every 10 seconds until fully melted.

Pour the melted chocolate into a squeeze bottle. Squeeze the chocolate over the parchment paper, making abstract shapes. Leave a bit of space between each shape, for easy removal. Place the tray in the freezer for about 2 hours. Once the chocolate is set, use a spatula to remove it from the parchment.

Chocolate abstracts may be stored for several days in the freezer between sheets of parchment paper.

When you are ready to serve dessert, scoop the ice cream into a bowl. Top with one of the chocolate decorations. Serve immediately, splashing amaretto over the ice cream at the table.

go team cupcakes

Makes about 18 cupcakes

Nothing says "fun" like cupcakes. Their popularity has skyrocketed in New York City, where numerous bakeries inspire block-long lines of eager cupcake connoisseurs. My recipe is adapted from my favorite cookbook of all time, *The Joy of Cooking*, which I've been using since I was a kid. It's a white-cake recipe that uses egg white instead of whole eggs—and just the right amount of butter. I'm proud to say I grew up on store-bought pudding and canned icing, so that's what I like best (not to mention the fact that they're quicker), but of course you can make your own, if you prefer.

1 box store-bought instant vanilla pudding

2½ cups cake flour, sifted before measuring

2½ teaspoons baking powder

½ teaspoon salt

8 tablespoons (1 stick) butter

1½ cups sugar

1 cup milk

1 teaspoon vanilla

5 egg whites

16-ounce can store-bought vanilla icing
   (or your favorite flavor)

Decorative sugar in your team's colors

Prepare the vanilla pudding according to package instructions and set aside.

Preheat the oven to 375°F and make sure all ingredients are at room temperature.

Resift the cake flour with the baking powder and salt and set aside in a large mixing bowl. In the bowl of an electric mixer, cream the butter and sugar until fluffy. Add one-third of the flour mixture to the butter mixture, then ⅓ cup milk, alternating until completely incorporated. Add the vanilla, stir, and remove the bowl from the mixer. In another bowl, whip the egg whites until stiff but still fluffy. Gently fold the egg whites into the batter.

Line a cupcake pan with paper or foil cupcake holders and fill each holder ¾ full with batter. Bake 20 to 25 minutes, or until the tops are golden and a toothpick inserted in the center comes out clean. Let cool.

To fill the cupcakes, cut a cone-shaped piece of cake out of the top of each cupcake and reserve the cones. Fill a pastry bag (or a plastic bag with a corner cut off) with the prepared pudding and squeeze a small amount into each cupcake. Replace the cones, ice the cupcakes, and finish them with your favorite team- or party-inspired garnish.

mary's lavender panna cotta

Serves 8

My colleague and friend Chef Mary Cleaver is at the forefront of the movement toward improving our food supply as a nation. She has taught me to strive to include as many organic, local, and seasonal ingredients as possible in my own cooking, and so I wanted to share one of her sweet recipes with you for a lovely summer dessert.

5 cups heavy cream

1⅓ cups milk

2 tablespoons dried lavender flowers

1½ cups sugar

Two ½-ounce packets powdered gelatin

Honey, for garnish

Combine the cream, 1 cup of the milk, and the lavender in a saucepan and bring it to a boil. Take the pan off the heat and stir in the sugar until it dissolves. Strain out the lavender.

While the cream mixture is cooling slightly, pour the remaining ⅓ cup cold milk into a small bowl and sprinkle the powdered gelatin over it. Let stand for 5 minutes. Stir the dissolved gelatin into the very warm cream mixture. (If it has become too cool to dissolve the gelatin, set it back on a low flame, stirring continuously, until the gelatin is completely incorporated into the cream.)

Pour the mixture into individual serving vessels or a single dish. Let sit for at least 6 hours in the refrigerator, undisturbed, on a flat surface. Drizzle the panna cotta lightly with a few drops of honey before serving.

It took me a long time to become a decent amateur mixologist (and I am always learning). Somehow, although cooking seems natural to me, the idea of balancing flavors in a cocktail was intimidating, and I couldn't remember any of the recipes or which ingredients went in which drinks. In fact, I was once forced to stand in for a sick bartender at a restau-

quaffs & quenchers

rant where I worked, and by the end of the night, I needed a drink myself. • Thanks to my friends and family, who all love a good cocktail (my sister Sara will try any fancy drink at least once), I now love to experiment with flavor combinations and twists on classic cocktails. In this section, you'll find the cocktails I think every good host should be familiar with, followed by the fun drinks we invented for the parties in this book.

martini
(gin or vodka)

Makes 1 cocktail

The key to a good martini is a restrained use of vermouth. Some bartenders like to joke that they merely wave the vermouth bottle over the glass to get the perfect balance.

A drop or two of extra-dry vermouth
3 ounces vodka or gin, well chilled
Lemon twist or olive garnish

Chill your glasses in the freezer. Drop the vermouth into the glass and swirl it to coat the glass. Add the chilled vodka or gin and your choice of lemon twist (rub the rim of the glass with the lemon before dropping it into the drink) or olives on a toothpick.

vodka gimlet

Makes 1 cocktail

You can make this drink with gin as well, but I prefer a really good vodka.

2 ounces vodka, well chilled
2 tablespoons Rose's lime juice

In a cocktail mixing glass filled with ice, combine the ingredients. Shake, strain, and serve "up" in a small cocktail glass.

tip

CHILL IT!

When it comes to martinis, colder is better. Keep your vodka and gin in the freezer (it won't totally freeze), and when you're ready for a cocktail, it will be ready for you.

hint

SOAK IT UP

You can soak your olives in a couple of tablespoons of vermouth for an hour or so, then simply add the olives, on a toothpick, to the drink in place of the drops of vermouth.

grand margarita

Makes 2 cocktails

This twist on the classic recipe is for when you're making margaritas in small quantities, as the fresh lime juice is a bit more work. I've added a splash of orange juice to pick up on the orange liqueur, but you can omit that if you like. See page 191 for my Margaritas Más Grandes recipe if you need a whole batch.

6 ounces tequila (use your favorite)

¼ cup fresh lime juice (2 limes)

2 ounces Simple Syrup (see right)
    or 2 tablespoons superfine sugar

1 tablespoon Grand Marnier

Splash orange juice (optional)

Salt for glasses (optional)

2 lime wedges, for garnish

In a cocktail shaker filled with ice, combine all the ingredients and shake. Strain and serve in salt-rimmed glasses garnished with lime wedges.

SIMPLE SYRUP

Makes about 1½ cups

Simple syrup is the bartender's secret ingredient for many cocktails, such as the Sazerac. It's so easy, and you can keep it in your refrigerator for about three weeks.

1 cup sugar

1 cup water

In a saucepan, combine the sugar and water and cook over low heat till the sugar dissolves. Let the syrup cool before using.

SALTING A GLASS

You can buy a salt rimmer from any store that sells good barware, but you can also just spread some salt on a bread plate, rub the rim of your cocktail glass with a cut lime wedge (to coat it in lime juice), then dip the rim in the salt. If you want to get creative, mix half sugar and half salt for a sweet-'n'-salty twist.

dark & stormy

Makes 1 cocktail

The Dark & Stormy originated in Bermuda, where it was made with ginger beer rather than ginger ale. The distinction bears mentioning, as ginger ale would seem a likely substitute. What's the difference? Ginger beer has a much stronger ginger flavor that can stand up to the fullness of the dark rum. It's worth the extra effort to find the real McCoy!

2 ounces dark rum, such as Gosling's
Juice of ½ lime
4 ounces Ginger beer

Fill a highball glass with ice. Pour the rum and lime juice into the glass, then add the ginger beer and stir to incorporate.

sazerac

Makes 4 cocktails

This is a classic New Orleans cocktail—jazzy and chic. My favorite of all time is mixed at the world-famous Antoine's in the French Quarter, where it is served in miniature old-fashioned glasses. This is the version I make at home. Feel free to use Pernod (a licorice-flavored French digestif) or absinthe, which is legal again and all the rage. For a true Sazerac, however, make sure to use Peychaud's Bitters. You can order it online or get it at a fine liquor store.

2 teaspoons simple syrup or superfine sugar
4 drops Peychaud's Bitters
4 drops Pernod or absinthe
8 ounces bourbon or rye whisky
4 lemon twists, for garnish

In a cocktail mixing glass, combine the syrup, bitters, and Pernod. Add a few ice cubes, then pour in the bourbon and stir. Strain into a small cocktail or old-fashioned glass. Rub the rim of the glass with the lemon twist and then garnish the drink with the twist.

kir royale

Makes 6 cocktails

Crème de cassis is a sweet, black currant–flavored liqueur. There are two basic types of kir cocktails. This recipe is for a kir royale, a lovely, bubbly blush aperitif. The other, a plain kir, is made with crisp, still white wine, and you can make it just the same way as the recipe below, substituting wine for the Champagne.

1 bottle (750 ml) Champagne
6 teaspoons crème de cassis

Pour the crème de cassis into each Champagne flute, then fill the glasses with Champagne. Serve immediately for best bubbles.

white wine spritzer

Makes 1 cocktail

Spritzers are among my favorite light drinks and are a great way to maximize the returns on a bottle of inexpensive, crisp white wine, such as Pinot Grigio. You should make them as you go, as the club soda should be bubbly, not flat.

5 ounces white wine
2 ounces club soda
Lemon twist

Pour the wine into a stem wine glass with a few ice cubes. Add the club soda and stir. Garnish with a lemon twist and serve right away.

manhattan

Makes 1 cocktail

Some Manhattan recipes call for rye whisky, but I prefer the caramel flavor and color of bourbon. The classic garnish for this is a maraschino cherry, but for a new twist, you could use a fresh cherry that's been soaked in Cherry Syrup (page 195).

2 ounces bourbon
1 ounce sweet vermouth
Dash of Angostura bitters
Maraschino cherry, for garnish

Pour all ingredients into a cocktail mixing glass filled with ice and stir. Strain into an "up" or martini glass (also called a cocktail glass). Garnish with a maraschino cherry.

tip

THE PERFECT MANHATTAN

A "perfect" Manhattan combines ½ ounce dry vermouth with ½ ounce sweet vermouth rather than using all sweet vermouth. Give it a try and see what combination you like best.

cosmopolitan

Makes 1 cocktail

2 ounces vodka
1 ounce Triple Sec
1 ounce cranberry juice
1½ teaspoons fresh lime juice
½ teaspoon lemon juice
1 lemon twist

In a cocktail shaker over ice, combine the vodka, Triple Sec, cranberry juice, lime and lemon juice, and shake well. Rub a lemon twist around the rim of a cocktail glass, and then toss it into the glass. Strain the mixture into the glass and serve immediately.

malik's tropical rosé sangria

Serves 6–8

Malik is the talented mixologist in my group of friends (he also happens to be my boyfriend!). He keeps frosty glasses ready in his freezer and invents cocktails upon request. This sangria is one of his best inventions. It's light, refreshing, and unique, as it uses rosé wine instead of white or red.

2 oranges, with peel, sliced into rounds

1 large apple, with peel, cored and cut into small pieces

1 cup fresh pineapple chunks

½ cup sugar or ¼ cup simple syrup

½ cup Grand Marnier

750 ml bottle fruity rosé wine (I suggest Tavel, Rosé d'Anjou, or Côtes de Provence)

1 cup pineapple juice

2 cups club soda or seltzer

Cut the orange rounds into quarters and put half of them in a large pitcher, along with the apple and pineapple chunks, sugar, and a splash of the Grand Marnier.

Add the wine, pineapple juice, and the remaining Grand Marnier. Stir well, then chill for at least a half hour to let the flavors come together. Just before serving, add the club soda. Pour into wine glasses over ice, if desired, making sure each glass gets chunks of the fruit as well as sangria. Garnish with the remaining orange wedges.

margaritas más grandes

Serves 10

This recipe is an easy crowd-pleaser. You can make it ahead of time and serve it in pitchers or old mason jars. You can also present it in one of the many fun drink dispensers out there.

2½ cups tequila

1 quart homemade or store-bought limeade

½ cup Grand Marnier

¼ cup fresh lime juice (2 limes)

2 limes, cut into wedges, for garnish

Salt for glasses (optional)

Mix all the liquids together in a large pitcher or serving vessel. Serve with a bucket of ice as well as lime wedges and a plate of salt on the side for garnishing glass rims, if desired.

rudolph fizz

Makes 6 cocktails

1 bottle (750 ml) of Prosecco or other sparkling wine

6 teaspoons Cherry Syrup (see page 195)

Fill a Champagne flute three-quarters full with the sparkling wine. Drop 1 teaspoon cherry syrup into each glass and serve.

lemon verbena vodka cooler

Makes 4 cocktails

Add a splash of club soda just before serving to give this cooler a little extra sparkle.

6 ounces vodka
2 cups pink grapefruit juice
1 cup lemonade
8 sprigs fresh lemon verbena

Combine the liquids in a pitcher, along with 4 sprigs of the lemon verbena. Let the mixture steep in your refrigerator for at least 1 hour and up to a day. Pour over ice and garnish each glass with a sprig of lemon verbena to add extra flavor.

french peach brunch punch

Makes 1 cocktail

3 ounces Lillet Blanc
2 ounces orange juice
2 ounces peach nectar
1 ounce club soda
Peach slice, for garnish

Mix all the ingredients together and serve over ice. Garnish with a fresh slice of peach.

plum wine spritzer

Makes 1 cocktail

Plum wine is available in Asian markets. Its earthy sweetness is nicely accented with the brightness of the orange juice and the fizz of the club soda.

4 ounces plum wine
2 ounces orange juice
2 ounces club soda

Pour the ingredients over ice and stir.

amaretto hot chocolate

Makes 1 hot chocolate drink

⅔ cup milk
5½ tablespoons good-quality Mexican cocoa
1 ounce amaretto
Whipped cream (optional)

In a saucepan over medium heat, warm the milk. Add the cocoa and stir. Remove from the heat and stir in the amaretto. Pour into a mug or glass and top with whipped cream, if you like.

pomegranate cherry sakejito

Makes 2 cocktails

This is, of course, a twist on the mojito. I've replaced the rum with sake and added a few unexpected flavors to create magic!

1 lime, quartered

2 tablespoons fresh mint leaves

1 teaspoon superfine sugar

4 ounces sake (use a light or smooth style, such as junmai or ginjo)

2 ounces pomegranate juice

1 tablespoon Cherry Syrup (see right)

2 ounces club soda

In each serving glass, muddle 2 lime quarters, half the mint, and half the sugar.

In a cocktail shaker filled with ice, mix the sake, pomegranate juice, and cherry syrup. Stir and strain into the serving glasses atop the lime and mint mixture. Divide the club soda between the two glasses, stir, and serve.

CHERRY SYRUP

Makes about 2¼ cups

This syrup is so easy to make and so versatile. You can use it in cocktails (the Rudolph Fizz, page 191, for example) or in kids' drinks (with orange juice, club soda, and a splash of syrup). You can mix it in with your favorite warm maple syrup for pancakes, waffles, or French toast, or drizzle it over ice cream. And, of course, it makes a great gift for your fellow foodies!

1 pound frozen dark sweet cherries

1 cup sugar

In a small saucepan over high heat, combine the ingredients with 2 cups water and stir. Bring the mixture to a boil, then reduce the heat to a simmer and cook for 20 minutes, or until the mixture thickens and reduces by about half.

Pour the mixture through a fine strainer, reserving the liquid and discarding the cherry skins. Refrigerate the syrup until ready to use (it should keep for several weeks).

NONALCOHOLIC QUENCHERS

Several cocktails in the previous section can be made nonalcoholic simply by leaving out the liquor component. The French Peach Brunch Punch (page 192), for example, would be great with club soda instead of bubbly. And the Rudolph Fizz (page 191) could be made with sparkling apple cider instead of Prosecco. However, you can't make a wine spritzer with no wine (unless you just want a glass of club soda with lemon!) so here are some more inspirations.

muddled berry lemonade

Serves 6–8

Try to get the best raspberries. Their tart sweetness will work beautifully with the lemonade.

1 cup fresh raspberries, rinsed and dried
1 cup fresh strawberries, tops removed, halved
1 handful fresh mint leaves, stems removed
½ gallon (64 ounces) sweetened pink lemonade (or substitute regular)

In the bottom of a pitcher, muddle the raspberries, strawberries, and mint leaves with a wooden spoon. Add the lemonade and stir. Serve over ice in sugar-rimmed glasses (see page 185 for how to coat a glass rim).

WHAT IS MUDDLING?

"Muddling" is a bartending term used to describe the act of crushing ingredients together (mainly fruits or herbs and sugars) in the bottom of a glass, thereby adding a fuller flavor to the drink. Sometimes the muddled ingredients are strained out, and sometimes, as in the case of a mojito or the lemonade above, they're left in as part of the presentation.

tunisian mint tea

Serves 8

I first sampled this delicious, very sweet tea in an outdoor café in Tunisia. Its intense flavor is balanced by the earthiness of the pine nuts. Feel free to adjust the sweetness to your own preference.

3 individual bags black tea (or the equivalent in loose tea)

¾ cups sugar, or to taste

2 large handfuls mint sprigs

2 tablespoons pine nuts, for garnish

In a saucepan, bring 2 cups of water to a boil. Remove the pan from the heat, add the sugar, and stir. Add the mint to the tea and pour the hot water over and let steep, off the heat, for at least 5 minutes.

Strain the tea to remove the mint. Serve warm or at room temperature in small glasses and garnish each glass with a few pine nuts.

frozen sunset

Makes 1 drink

2 scoops lemon sorbet

8 ounces pomegranate juice

4 ounces blood orange juice

2 ounces peach nectar

2 slices blood orange for serving

In a blender, mix all ingredients except the orange slices and blend on low speed. Pour into highball glasses and serve with a straw and a slice of blood orange for garnish.

acknowledgments

Producing a book about parties entails even more effort and expertise than producing the parties themselves. I have so many wonderful people to honor for their contributions and for their help in bringing this book to life. It is truly a dream come true for me and I am very grateful.

First and foremost, I must thank my events director, Nicole Fazzini, without whose help in organizing, shepherding, and motivating our team, this project could never have happened, especially considering the fact that in between photo shoots we have a bustling events business to run. Nicole, your can-do spirit and relentless attention to detail are an inspiration to me.

Next, I owe a huge thank-you to the incredibly talented and wonderful William Geddes, who captured the beautiful images of the parties, food, interiors, and details in this book. I am grateful also to Bill's fantastic assistants, Jeremy Lips and Ryan Joseph for their fine work and their fun company.

We were privileged to set our parties in some gorgeous homes, and I must thank those who made these locations accessible. I'm deeply grateful to Sue MacKenzie, Lori Klipstein, and Jerry O'Connor of O'Connor Capital for making all our parties at the super-stylish Manhattan House so enjoyable. To Marianna Klaiman at the Athena Group, thank you for your hospitality at 111 Central Park North and at the A in Jersey City. Karen Lashinsky opened her beautiful residence at 632 on Hudson to us, and Julie North and Will Fogg welcomed us into their stunning loft in Tribeca. Even my brother, David Bussen, let our whole team take over his kitchen and his backyard on more than one occasion—thank you all so much.

I am beyond grateful to everyone at Bloomindgales, but I cannot thank Hannah Soule, registry manager here in New York, enough for her help in creating the tabletop looks for many of the parties on these pages. Bloomingdales has been a fantastic resource throughout the process of making this book (can you imagine being able to borrow anything you like—Versace china, Faberge cocktail shakers—for your next party?) and Hannah and company made the whole experience enjoyable and easy.

To my fabulous food styling interns, Michele Humes and Nathan Slusser, big hugs and lots of cocktails! These two talented pros helped to tweak and test recipes and cooked with much creativity for long hours, not to mention preparing food in places where we weren't always allowed to use the million-dollar kitchens. Thank you both for your hard work and creativity. For their research assistance on details for the resource guide, I'd like to thank Eliza Coleman and our intern Gina Palazzo.

As always, I am in awe of and indebted to Leslie Stoker, my publisher at Stewart, Tabori & Chang. Leslie, thank you for believing in the Simple Stunning message, and for your commitment to creating great books. I probably owe my editor, Jennifer Levesque, an apology or two in addition to my thanks for enlisting our charmingly brutal copyeditor, Ana Deboo, who, as my dad would say, doesn't sugar-coat it. I am grateful to you both for your expertise and efforts to whip this book into shape! Thanks are also due to Kate Norment for keeping the project (and me!) on track.

To Joy Tutela and David Black at the David Black Literary Agency, thank you forever for all your guidance.

To my friend and colleague, Marta Tracy, I feel lucky to know you and to benefit from your wisdom. Wendy Crispell, thanks for your friendship and your input on the Raising the Bar chapter.

Susi Oberhelman, my lovely and talented book designer, how can I thank you? From the beginning of our collaboration, you instantly captured the Simple Stunning vibe in your designs and brought the ideas to life with your layouts.

It takes a village to make me look good. To Jacqui Phillips of the Jacqueline Pasquale Spa, Julio Sandino of Nars, and to Vincent Roppatte and Deborah Wynn at Saks Fifth Avenue, thank you for your hair and makeup artistry.

Much love and gratitude to my sister Sara, her husband Samir, and my little nephew Kiran for being a wonderful family. Many thanks to all my clients, an amazing group of gracious party hosts and hostesses, along with my mother, Linda Mikhael, who have taught me so much about how to entertain in style.

Finally, to Malik, thank you for making every day feel like a reason to celebrate.

resources

Visit us at **www.karenbussen.com** for more products and links.

COPYRIGHT PAGE

Glass candlesticks:
Crate & Barrel
www.crateandbarrel.com

Glass vases:
Jamali Garden
www.jamaligarden.com

CONTENTS PAGE

Vase:
Crate & Barrel
www.crateandbarrel.com

Pink votives:
Jamali Garden
www.jamaligarden.com

ADVICE FOR THE HOST

PAGE 15
Green kitchen accessories:
Crate & Barrel
www.crateandbarrel.com

Sangria pitcher and glasses:
Target
www.target.com

YOUR PARTY PANTRY

PAGE 21
Napkin rings:
Bloomingdales
www.bloomingdales.com

PAGE 23
White vases:
IKEA
www.IKEA-USA.com

RAISING THE BAR

Location:
Manhattan House
200 East 66th Street
New York, NY 10065
212-566-0660
www.manhattanhouse.com

PAGE 24-31
Decanters, glassware & china:
Bloomingdales
www.bloomingdales.com

PAGE 31
Stainless steel wine glass clip:
Chef Central
www.chefcentral.com

CREATING AMBIENCE

PAGE 34
Place setting:
Bloomingdales
www.bloomingdales.com

PAGE 34
Asian centerpiece accents:
Pearl River
www.pearlriver.com

PAGE 37
All candles:
Jamali Garden
www.jamaligarden.com

PAGE 38
Red lanterns and red flatware:
Christmas Tree Shops
www.christmastreeshops.com

Dinner plates:
IKEA
www.IKEA-USA.com

LATIN SPICE

Location:
111 Central Park North
New York, NY 10026
212-459-0200
www.theathenagroup.com

PAGE 44
Post-it flags:
Staples
www.staples.com

PAGE 45
Serving platters:
Target
www.target.com

Chinese spoons:
Pearl River
www.pearlriver.com

Pillows and vases:
IKEA
www.IKEA-USA.com

PAGE 46
Candles and rattan tray:
Target
www.target.com

WINE & CHEESE TASTING

Location:
632 on Hudson
632 Hudson Street
New York, NY 10014
212-620-7631
www.632onhudson.com

PAGE 49

Fondue pot:
IKEA
www.IKEA-USA.com

Mini chalkboards:
Michaels
www.michaels.com

Serving platter and plates:
Bloomingdales
www.bloomingdales.com

Cutting board and cheese accessories:
Sur La Table
www.surlatable.com

PAGE 52

China and glassware:
Bloomingdales
www.bloomingdales.com

Stainless steel wine glass clip:
Chef Central
www.chefcentral.com

HOLIDAY TOAST

Location:
Private home

PAGE 54

Pastries and petits fours:
Payard Patisserie & Bistro
www.payard.com

PAGE 55

Ornaments:
Target
www.target.com

**All furnishings, glassware, coasters
& mirrored tiles:**
IKEA
www.IKEA-USA.com

PAGE 56

Champagne flutes:
Bloomingdales
www.bloomingdales.com

PAGE 59

Mirrored ball ornaments:
Jamali Garden
www.jamaligarden.com

ZEN LADIES' NIGHT

Location:
Private Home

PAGE 63

China, crystal, flatware:
Bloomingdales
www.bloomingdales.com

Centerpiece bowls and Asian accents:
Pearl River
www.pearlriver.com

Candles:
Jamali Garden
www.jamaligarden.com

Asian rubber stamp:
Michaels
www.michaels.com

PAGE 64

Sea grass mats:
Pearl River
www.pearlriver.com

Asian rubber stamps:
Michaels
www.michaels.com

Teapot and cups:
Sur La Table
www.surlatable.com

GLOBAL POTLUCK

Location:
Private home

PAGE 66

Small suitcase:
Michaels
www.michaels.com

Flatware:
Bloomingdales
www.bloomingdales.com

PAGE 67

Chinese lanterns:
Pearl River
www.pearlriver.com

Tagine:
Sur La Table
www.surlatable.com

**Glassware, votive holders,
rubber tile place mats, serving bowls,
and platters:**
Bloomingdales
www.bloomingdales.com

Rubber stamp and craft paper:
Michaels
www.michaels.com

PAGE 68

Craft supplies:
Michaels
www.michaels.com

PAGE 69

Serving tray:
Bloomingdales
www.bloomingdales.com

Indian sweets:
Sukhadia's
www.sukhadia.com

GAME NIGHT GET-TOGETHER

Location:
Manhattan House
(see page 200 for contact information)

PAGE 71

All tableware:
Bloomingdales
www.bloomingdales.com

WEIGHT EQUIVALENTS

The metric weights given in this chart are not exact equivalents, but have been rounded up or down slightly to make measuring easier.

Avoirdupois	Metric
¼ oz	7 g
½ oz	15 g
1 oz	30 g
2 oz	60 g
3 oz	90 g
4 oz	115 g
5 oz	150 g
6 oz	175 g
7 oz	200 g
8 oz (½ lb)	225 g
9 oz	250 g
10 oz	300 g
11 oz	325 g
12 oz	350 g
13 oz	375 g
14 oz	400 g
15 oz	425 g
16 oz (1 lb)	450 g
1½ lb	750 g
2 lb	900 g
2¼ lb	1 kg
3 lb	1.4 kg
4 lb	1.8 kg

VOLUME EQUIVALENTS

These are not exact equivalents for American cups and spoons, but have been rounded up or down slightly to make measuring easier.

American	Metric	Imperial
¼ tsp	1.2 ml	
½ tsp	2.5 ml	
1 tsp	5.0 ml	
½ Tbsp (1.5 tsp)	7.5 ml	
1 Tbsp (3 tsp)	15 ml	
¼ cup (4 Tbsp)	60 ml	2 fl oz
⅓ cup (5 Tbsp)	75 ml	2.5 fl oz
½ cup (8 Tbsp)	125 ml	4 fl oz
⅔ cup (10 Tbsp)	150 ml	5 fl oz
¾ cup (12 Tbsp)	175 ml	6 fl oz
1 cup (16 Tbsp)	250 ml	8 fl oz
1¼ cups	300 ml	10 fl oz (½ pint)
1½ cups	350 ml	12 fl oz
2 cups (1 pint)	500 ml	16 fl oz
2½ cups	625 ml	20 fl oz (1 pint)
1 quart	1 liter	32 fl oz

OVEN TEMPERATURE EQUIVALENTS

Oven Mark	F	C	Gas
Very cool	250–275	130–140	½–1
Cool	300	150	2
Warm	325	170	3
Moderate	350	180	4
Moderately hot	375	190	5
	400	200	6
Hot	425	220	7
	450	230	8
Very hot	475	250	9

index